FAMOUS MEN OF
ANCIENT ROME
Lives of Julius Caesar, Nero,
Marcus Aurelius and Others

FAMOUS MEN OF
ANCIENT ROME
Lives of Julius Caesar, Nero,
Marcus Aurelius and Others

JOHN H. HAAREN AND
A. B. POLAND

DOVER PUBLICATIONS, INC.
Mineola, New York

Bibliographical Note

This Dover edition, first published in 2005, is an unabridged republication of *Famous Men of Rome,* originally published by American Book Company, New York, 1904.

Library of Congress Cataloging-in-Publication Data

Haaren, John H. (John Henry), 1855–1916.
    [Famous men of Rome]
    Famous men of ancient Rome : lives of Julius Caesar, Nero, Marcus Aurelius and others / John H. Haaren and A.B. Poland.
        p. cm.
    "An unabridged republication of Famous men of Rome, originally published by American Book Company, New York, 1904."
    ISBN-13: 978-0-486-44361-4
    ISBN-10: 0-486-44361-2
    1. Rome—Biography—Juvenile literature. 2. Rome—History—Juvenile literature. I. Poland, Addison B. II. Title.

DG203.H26 2005
920.037—dc22
[B]
                                                            2005045421

Manufactured in the United States by Courier Corporation
44361202
www.doverpublications.com

Preface

The study of history, like the study of a landscape, should begin with the most conspicuous features. Not until these have been fixed in memory will the lesser features fall into their appropriate places and assume their right proportions.

In order to attract and hold the child's attention, each conspicuous feature of history presented to him should have an individual for its center. The child identifies himself with the personage presented. It is not Romulus or Hercules or Cæsar or Alexander that the child has in mind when he reads, but himself, acting under the prescribed conditions.

Prominent educators, appreciating these truths, have long recognized the value of biography as a preparation for the study of history and have given it an important place in their schools.

The former practice in many elementary schools of beginning the detailed study of American history without any previous knowledge of general history limited the pupil's range of vision, restricted his sympathies, and left him without material for comparisons. Moreover, it denied to him a knowledge of his inheritance from the Greek philosopher, the Roman lawgiver, the Teutonic lover of freedom. Hence the recommendation so strongly urged in the report of the Committee of Ten—and emphasized, also, in the report of the Committee of Fifteen—that the study of Greek, Roman, and modern European history in the form of biography should precede the study of detailed American history in our elementary schools. The Committee of Ten recommends an eight years' course in history, beginning with the fifth year in school and continuing to the end of the high school course. The first two years of this course are given wholly to the study of biography and mythology. The Committee of Fifteen recommends that history be taught in all the grades of the elementary school and emphasizes the value of biography and of general history.

The series of historical stories to which this volume belongs was prepared in conformity with the foregoing recommendations and with the best practice of leading schools.

Teachers often find it impracticable to give to the study of mythology and biography a place of its own in an already overcrowded curriculum. In such cases they prefer to correlate history with reading and for this purpose the volumes of this series supply most desirable text-books. It has been the aim of the authors to make an interesting story of each man's life and to tell these stories in a style so simple that pupils in the lower grades will read them with pleasure, and so dignified that they may be used with profit as text-books for reading.

Contents

ROMULUS

I

Many, many years ago, in the pleasant land of Italy, there was a little city called Alba. It stood on the sunny side of a mountain, near the River Tiber and not far from the Mediterranean Sea. In this city and around the mountain lived a brave, intelligent people known as Latins. Several other tribes inhabited the adjacent mountains and plains.

The Latins were ruled by kings, and one of their kings in very early times was named Æ-ne'as. He was a famous Trojan chief who had come over the seas to Italy and settled there with his family and friends after Troy was destroyed by the Greeks.

A great many years after the death of Æneas one of his descendants named Pro'cas was king of Alba. He ruled wisely and well for a long time, and his rather small kingdom on the mountain side, with its wheat-fields and vineyards, was very prosperous. He had two sons, one named Nu'mi-tor, and the other A-mu'li-us. As Numitor was the elder he was heir to his father's throne, but when King Procas died Amulius seized the kingdom by force and made himself king.

Then Numitor, with his two children, a boy and a girl, left the king's palace at Alba and went to reside on a farm a short distance away.

II

Amulius was now king, but he did not feel quite happy. He was much troubled about Numitor's son and daughter.

1

The son, he thought, might some day claim the right to be king as heir of his father, or the daughter might marry and have a son who could become king as grandchild of Numitor.

To prevent either of these things from happening Amulius had Numitor's son secretly put to death, and he appointed the daughter Syl'vi-a to be a priestess, or an attendant, in the temple of the goddess Ves'ta. Only young girls were appointed attendants in this temple, and they had to take a vow that they would not marry for thirty years. They were called Vestal Virgins. It was their duty to keep a fire burning continually on the altar of the goddess. This was called the Sacred Fire, and it was believed that if it went out some great disaster would happen to the city.

Amulius now thought there was nothing to hinder him from being king of Alba all his life. But one day the god Mars came down to the city from his palace on a high mountain top and saw Sylvia as she went out of the temple to get water at a well. He fell deeply in love with her. She also fell in love with the god, for he had the appearance of a handsome young man. They were married secretly, and in course of time Sylvia had beautiful twin boys. When Amulius heard of this he gave orders that Sylvia should be put to death for breaking her vow and that the two infants should be thrown into the Tiber. These wicked orders were carried out, for no one dared to disobey the king.

Fortunately, however, the babes had been placed in a stout basket, which floated along the Tiber until it was carried by the waters to the foot of a hill called Pal'a-tine Hill. Here the huge roots of a wild fig-tree upset the basket, and the little ones were thrown out upon the river bank.

At this moment a great she-wolf came strolling down the hill to drink at the river's edge. She heard the feeble cries of the infants and went to the place where they lay helpless on the wet sands. She touched them gently with her rough paws, turned them over and licked their faces and plump bodies. Perhaps she thought they were some of her own cubs. At any rate, she carried the babes up the hill to her cave under a large rock. There she fed them as she fed her own cubs and seemed pleased to have them near her. It is said that a woodpecker flew in and out of the cave many times a day, bringing berries for the boys to eat.

One morning as Faus'tu-lus, the herdsman of King Amulius, was going over Palatine Hill looking for cattle that had gone astray he saw the boys playing with the wolf at the mouth of her cave. He frightened the wolf away and took the boys to his home. His wife pitied the little foundlings and cared for them as though they were her own children.

The herdsman named them Rom'u-lus and Re'mus. They grew up to be strong, handsome youths, brave and kind. Until they were twenty years old they lived with the herdsman and helped him in his work, and roamed over the hills light-hearted and free.

During all these years Numitor lived on his farm, and his brother Amulius remained king of Alba. Numitor did not know that his two grandsons had been saved from a watery grave and were liviing so near to him.

But one day Remus had a quarrel with some of the herdsmen of Numitor and they took him prisoner. They then brought him before Numitor, who was much impressed with the noble appearance of the youth and asked him who he was.

Remus told all he knew about himself and Romulus; how they had been found at the cave of the she-wolf and had been reared by the king's herdsman. Just then Faustulus and Romulus came searching for Remus, and were full of joy when they found that no harm had come to him. Numitor questioned the herdsman about the finding of the twins, and after hearing his story was convinced that Romulus and Remus were Sylvia's boys, who had been strangely saved from the wrath of their cruel uncle. He was very happy at finding his grandsons and he thanked the herdsman for his good care of them.

Romulus and Remus were also very happy at finding a grandfather and at the sudden change of their fortune. When they were told about Amulius and his wicked deeds, they resolved to punish him for the murder of their mother. So with a few followers they rushed to the palace at Alba and entered the king's chamber.

"Behold! we are Sylvia's sons whom you thought you had killed," they shouted to Amulius, as he started up in alarm at their entrance. "You killed our mother and you shall die for it."

Before he could utter a word they sprang on him with drawn swords and cut his head off. Then they brought Numitor to the palace, and the people welcomed him as the rightful king of Alba.

III

After a little time the two brothers thought they would build a city on Palatine Hill, where the she-wolf had nursed them. So they went to the hill and selected a site. Then they began to talk of a name for their city.

"I will be king and give the new city my name," said Romulus.

"No," cried Remus. "I will be the king and name the city after myself. I have just as much right as you have."

So the brothers argued for a while, but at last they agreed to settle the matter in this way:

At midnight Romulus was to stand on Palatine Hill, and Remus was to stand on another hill a short distance off. Then they were to ask the gods to show them a sign of favor in the sky, and the first who should see anything very remarkable was to name the new city and be its king.

So they went to watch, but nothing appeared until sunrise of the second day, when Remus saw six great vultures flying across the sky from north to south. He ran swiftly to Palatine Hill and told Romulus of what he had seen. But just then twelve vultures, one after another, flew high over the head of Romulus in an almost unbroken line and were soon lost to view.

Then Romulus claimed that he had the favor of the gods, as more birds had appeared to him, but Remus claimed that the gods favored him, as the birds had appeared to him first. Romulus asked the opinion of some of his friends, and as they all agreed that he was right in his claim he paid no further attention to Remus, but began to lay out the new city. He gave it the name of Roma, or Rome, after himself. With a plow he marked out the space on Palatine Hill and along the banks of the Tiber, and he built a low wall round about to protect the city from invaders.

One day while the work was going on Remus came by in a very bitter mood. He was still angry with Romulus. He laughed scornfully at the little wall and said to his brother:

"Shall such a defence as this keep your city? It may prevent children from getting in, but not men, for they can jump over it."

So saying, Remus put his hands on the wall and sprang over it, to show that his words were true. Romulus, in a sudden outburst of rage, struck him on the head with a spade and instantly killed him, at the same time crying out:

"So perish any one who shall hereafter attempt to leap over my wall."

Then Romulus continued his work. While he was building his wall he also built some houses. The first houses were nothing more than wood huts covered with mud and straw. But in course of time the Romans had houses of stone, and they built fine temples and theatres and streets and squares, and at last Rome became the greatest and grandest city in the whole world.

IV

Romulus founded Rome in the year 753 B.C. After he had built his city he had some difficulty in getting people to live in it. He had only a few followers and was not able to obtain any more. He decided, therefore, to make Rome a place of refuge, to which people who had got into trouble in other countries might come for safety.

And so when those who had committed crime in other places, and had to flee to escape punishment, found out that Romulus would give them a refuge, they came in large numbers to his city. People also came who had been driven from home by enemies, or had run away for one reason or another. It was not long, therefore, until Rome was full of men. There were men from many different tribes and countries. Thus the Roman nation began, and for years it steadily grew and prospered.

But the Romans were much troubled about one thing. A great many of them had no wives, and they could not get any, because the women of the neighboring tribes would not marry them, for the Romans had a bad name. Romulus was very anxious that his people should have good wives, but how they should get them greatly puzzled him for a long time. At last he hit upon a plan and began at once to carry it out.

He sent messengers to the cities all around to announce that on a certain day a great festival in honor of the god Ju'pi-ter would be held on the plain in front of Rome. There were to be games, combats, horse-racing, and other sports. The people were invited to attend the festival and also to take part in the contests for the prizes.

When the festival day came a multitude of men and women from far and near assembled before the walls of Rome. Hundreds of pretty girls were there in fine dresses. A great many came from the Sā'bine tribe. This was a tribe of warriors that lived on a mountain near Rome.

Suddenly Romulus blew a loud blast upon a horn. Then, quick as a flash, the Romans seized the girls and bore them off to Rome.

The Sabines were greatly enraged at this, and their king, Ti'tus Ta'ti-us, raised a large army and at once began a war against the Romans. The war went on for three years, but the Sabines were so strong that Romulus could not defeat them in the field. He therefore withdrew his army into the city. King Tatius quickly marched after him, resolved to take Rome or perish in the attempt.

Now Romulus had erected a strong fortress on a hill near the Palatine, to keep invaders from Rome. The hill was called the Sa-tur'ni-an Hill, and the fortress was in charge of a brave Roman captain, who had a daughter named Tar-pe'i-a.

When the Sabines reached this fortress they could go no further. They marched up and down seeking for a spot where they might force an entrance, but they could find none. There was a small, barred gate in the fortress, and through this gate Tarpeia came out to get water. King Tatius saw her. He at once stepped forward and said:

"Fair maiden, open the gate and let us in. If you do you shall have for your reward anything you ask."

Tarpeia was gazing with admiration at the bracelets of gold which the Sabines wore on their arms.

"I will open the gate," said she, "if you will give me some of those things which your soldiers wear upon their arms."

King Tatius agreed, and Tarpeia opened the gate. As the Sabines strode past the silly maiden each threw at her, not his bracelet, but his shield.

The shield then used was round or oblong and made of bronze, or of wicker-work or ox-hide covered with metal plates. It had two handles at the back, and the soldier held it with his left hand and arm so that he could move it up or down to save his head or breast from blows.

Tarpeia stood in amazement as the heavy shields began to pile up around her. One struck her, and then another and another. At last she fell to the ground and was soon crushed to death.

When the soldiers saw that Tarpeia was dead, they took up the shields they had thrown at her. Then they hurled her body from the top of a great rock that was near the gate she had opened. The rock was afterwards known as the Tarpeian Rock, and for hundreds of years the punishment for traitors in Rome was to be thrown from this rock.

As soon as they passed the fortress the Sabines ran down the Saturnian Hill to make an attack on Rome. But Romulus and his band of warriors bravely came out of the city to drive back the enemy. The two forces met in the valley, and then a fierce battle began.

But while they were fighting a crowd of excited women came running from the city. They were the Sabine women whom the Romans had carried off. Some of them had their infants in their arms and they rushed between the lines of soldiers and begged that the fight should stop.

"Do not fight any more for us," they said to their fathers and brothers. "We love the Romans we have married. They have been good to us, and we do not wish to leave them."

Of course, this settled the matter. Romulus had a talk with King Tatius, and they agreed not to fight any more. They also agreed that the two nations should be as one. They joined their governments and their armies, and each of the kings had equal power.

Soon afterwards King Tatius died. Then Romulus ruled alone for nearly forty years. He was a wise and just king and did a great deal of good for his people. He established a body called the Senate, to help him in important affairs of government. It was called the Senate from *senex*, the Latin word for an *old man*. It was formed of the chiefs or *old men* of the earliest settlers in Rome. The descendants of those settlers were called *patricians*, or fathers, from the Latin word *pater*, a father. They were the nobles, or upper class, in Rome. The ordinary citizens were called *plebeians*, from *plebs*, the Latin word for the *common people*.

Romulus took care to train up the young Romans to be good soldiers. Outside the city, along the bank of the Tiber, there was a great plain which in later times was called Cam'pus Mar'ti-us, or Field of Mars. Here the Roman soldiers were drilled. They were taught how to use the spear and the javelin and the sword and the shield. They were also exercised in running and jumping, and wrestling and swimming, and carrying heavy loads. Thus the young men were made fit to bear the hardships of war and to fight and win battles for their country.

It is related that in his old age Romulus suddenly disappeared from the earth. He called his people together on a great field one day, and while he was speaking to them a violent storm came on. The rain fell in torrents, and the lightning and thunder were so terrible that the people fled to their homes.

When the storm was over the people went back to the field, but Romulus was nowhere to be found. Then it was said that his father, the god Mars, had taken him up to the clouds in a golden chariot.

Next morning at early dawn a Roman citizen named Ju'li-us saw a figure descending from the heavens. It had the appearance of Romulus, and it approached Julius and said:

"Go and tell my people that it is the will of the gods that Rome shall be the greatest city of the world. Let them be brave and warlike, and no human power shall be able to conquer them."

Afterwards the Romans worshiped Romulus as a god. They worshiped him under the name Quir'i-nus, which was one of the names of the god Mars, and they built a temple to him on a hill which was called the Quir'i-nal Hill.

NUMA POMPILIUS

I

For a year after the disappearance of Romulus there was no king of Rome. The city was ruled by the Senate. But the people were not satisfied. They preferred to be ruled by one man, and, though they had the right to elect a king themselves, they left the choice to the Senate. The Senate chose Nu'ma Pom-pil'i-us, a very good and wise man, who belonged to the nation of the Sabines.

The first thing that Numa did after learning that he had been chosen king was to consult the augurs, to find out if it was the will of the gods that he should be the ruler of Rome.

The augurs were what we should call fortune-tellers. A number of them lived in Rome. They were much respected and occupied a large temple at the expense of the public. They pretended that by watching the sky and observing how birds and animals acted they could tell what would happen to people and to nations. Then when they were alone they would have a great deal of fun over the tricks they played upon the foolish people.

Numa made many important changes at the very beginning of his rule. Before he came to the throne Roman young men were brought up to no business but war. It was considered disgraceful for a Roman citizen, whether rich or poor, to work at any trade or manufacture. The slaves, who were persons taken prisoners in wars, did all the hard work. They made all the clothing, tools, arms, and household articles. They cooked and served the meals, and were general servants for the Roman families. Roman citizens might, however, without being degraded work on farms and vineyards, and many of them made their living in this way.

Shortly after King Numa began his reign he divided some of the public lands into small farms and gave one of these farms to every poor Roman. The public lands were lands that belonged to the nation and not to private persons.

It was rather hard at first for the new-made farmers to be contented on their farms and to do good work. They were mostly soldiers and had very little knowledge of anything except marching and fighting. But it was not long before they began to understand what a blessing it is to be self-supporting and independent. Their little farms were pleasant homes. They began to love their new life and soon were able to raise enough for the support of themselves and their families, with something to spare.

II

King Numa made many good laws. These laws were engraved on tablets of brass and at certain times were read and explained to the people by lawyers.

Numa was very friendly with the people of the countries surrounding Rome. He gave them help in times of trouble and would never listen to any talk of war with them. During the many years that he was king Rome had no enemies and no wars.

In a sacred grove, just outside the walls of Rome, there lived in a handsome grotto, or cavern, a beautiful woman named E-ge'ri-a. Some persons called her a goddess, while others thought she was a fairy. She seemed to have a great knowledge of magic and could do wonderful things. Whenever she called to the song-birds they would come flying around her. They would also perch on her head and shoulders and hands, and sing their sweetest songs. Even the fierce animals of the woods were her friends, and great bears and wolves would lie at her feet for hours and purr like cats.

This mysterious woman-goddess, or fairy, or whatever she was, greatly loved and honored good King Numa, and at last they were married. Then she taught him many of the magical secrets she possessed. He carefully studied the lessons she gave him, and in time he was able to do wonderful things himself.

III

The Romans were earnest worshipers of the gods and goddesses. They believed that there were many such beings, and they had many grand temples for religious service.

King Numa always paid great attention to religion. He appointed a large number of officials to take care of the temples, and to see that all the sacred ceremonies were properly carried out. He was constant and faithful in his own worship and thus, by his example, gradually induced the whole Roman people to become attentive to their religion.

The greatest of the gods that the Romans believed in was the god Jupiter. He was supposed to rule both the sky and the earth. He was so powerful that he could send thunderbolts from the heavens, and make the earth tremble by his nod. He had a wife named Ju'no who had a great deal to do with managing the affairs of the earth. It was at one time believed that Jupiter resided with many other gods on the top of a high mountain in Greece. This mountain was so thickly covered by clouds that the gods could not be seen. But they could see everything that took place on the earth.

Jupiter had two brothers named Nep'tune and Plu'to. Neptune was the god of the sea. He lived in a grand, golden palace at the bottom of the Mediterranean. He ruled everything under and upon the waters of the world. Now and then he sailed over the ocean in a grand chariot drawn by large fish called dolphins. When he was angry he caused the sea to rise in huge waves.

Pluto, the other brother of Jupiter, was the god of Hā'des, or the land of the dead. His home was far down in the earth, where all was dark and gloomy. The Romans believed that when people died they were borne away to the gloomy kingdom of Pluto.

The other principal gods were Mars, Mer'cu-ry, Vul'can, A-pol'lo, and Ja'nus.

Mars was the god of war, and was especially honored in Rome because it was believed that he was the father of Romulus. Certain days of the year were made festival days in his honor, and then there were splendid processions, songs of praise, and religious dances.

Mercury, the son of Jupiter, was the god of eloquence and commerce. He was also the messenger of the other gods. He was generally represented as flying swiftly through the air, carrying messages from place to place. On his head and feet were small wings, and in his hand he bore a golden staff with serpents twined around it.

Vulcan was a skillful worker in metals. He had a great forge in the heart of a burning mountain, where he made wonderful things of iron, copper, and gold. He looked after the welfare of blacksmiths, coppersmiths, and goldsmiths, and was their special god.

Apollo, also called Phœ'bus, which meant the sun, was the god of day. He gave light and heat to the world. He was also the god of music, archery, and medicine. His sister Di-a'na was the moon goddess or goddess of the night. She was also the goddess of hunting. In pictures she is sometimes represented with a quiver of arrows over her shoulder and holding a stag by the horns.

The god Janus was very much honored by the Romans. It was believed that this god presided over the beginning of every undertaking, and so when the Romans began any important work or business they prayed first to Janus. For this reason the first month or beginning of the year was called the month of Janus, or *January*. Janus was also the god of gates and doors. In statuary and pictures he is often shown with two faces looking in opposite directions, because every door faces two ways—outward and inward.

Numa Pompilius built a temple in honor of Janus. The door of this temple was always open in time of war, as a sign that the god had gone out to help the Romans. In time of peace the door was shut.

The Romans also believed in Ve'nus, the goddess of love; Mi-ner'va, the goddess of wisdom; Flora, the goddess of flowers, and many others.

The Romans had no special day, such as our Sunday, for religious service, but their temples (except the temple of Janus) were open every day. They had prayers and songs, and sometimes what they called sacred dances. They also made offerings to the gods, such as fruits or vegetables, and oxen, lambs, or goats. The offerings went finally into the hands of the priests of the temples.

Numa Pompilius reigned for nearly half a century, and under him the Romans were a peaceful, prosperous, and happy people.

THE HORATII AND THE CURIATII

I

The third king of Rome was Tul'lus Hos-til'i-us. In his reign a remarkable combat took place between three Roman brothers and three Latin brothers. The combat came about in this way:

For years the people of Rome and the people of Alba, also called Latins, as has been already said, were continually quarreling. They would invade and plunder each other's lands. At last, after many petty contests, war was declared between the two nations.

King Tullus marched the Roman army to the border of Alba, but here his progress was stopped by a great force of Latins, under the command of Met'ti-us, the Alban king.

Tullus looked at the strong lines of Latin soldiers, standing firm and resolute to resist the advance of the Romans, and thought that it might be well to have a talk with Mettius to see whether they could not agree on some way of settling the quarrel without a fight between the two armies. So he sent for Mettius and they talked the matter over. Mettius also wished very much to avoid a battle, and he said to Tullus:

"Would it not be well to fight in such a way that only a few of our soldiers would be killed instead of many? My plan is this: You shall select three of the best fighting men in the Roman army, and I will select the best three in the army of Alba. The six men shall fight in the presence of the two armies. If the Romans win Alba will submit to

15

Rome; but if the Latins win then Rome must submit to Alba. What say you to the plan?"

"It is a good one," said King Tullus, "and I agree to it. May the best men win!"

With these words they separated, and went to prepare for the combat on which was to depend the fate of the two nations.

II

The Romans selected as their champions three brothers belonging to a family known as the Horatius family. The brothers were called the Ho-ra'ti-i because this word is the plural form of Horatius. The Horatii brothers were tall, handsome men, with wonderful strength, endurance, and courage.

The Albans also selected three brothers as their champions. They were called the Cu-ri-a'ti-i. They were bold, skillful soldiers, famous for manly beauty and strength, and were champions well worthy to fight for a nation.

When all was ready the Horatii and the Curiatii advanced to the centre of a large field and took their places. They carried short, thick swords and large, round shields made of stout leather and metal. The two armies gathered around the six champions, but at a distance, so as to leave them plenty of room to fight.

There was silence for a few moments, and then the shrill notes of a trumpet rang out as a signal for the battle. Clash! clang! went the swords upon the shields, and the fight began.

Quick, skillful blows were given for a short time, but no one was seriously hurt. Suddenly the Latins shouted in intense excitement. Lo! one of the Horatii, after a fierce struggle with one of the Curiatii, was stricken down dead! The Romans groaned, hung their heads, and looked in anxious doubt at their remaining two champions.

Bravely the Horatii stood—two to three—and fought with all their might. Step by step they drove the Curiatii back across the field. Cheers rang out from the Romans at this heroic effort. The victory might yet be theirs!

But alas! one of the Curiatii, with a swift, sly sword-thrust, killed another of the Horatii. Then the Latins shouted:

"We have won! We have won! We have won! Hail to the brave Curiatii!"

The Romans were wild with grief and rage. They had now but one champion left—Horatius, the last of the heroic Horatii—and he was running from the field, as if he had given up the fight. He was followed by the Curiatii, though they were all wounded. One of them, running ahead of the others, came up to Horatius and was raising his sword when the Roman turned upon him quickly and slew him.

The cries of the two armies were now hushed, as if by magic. All eyes were upon the champions, and there was a painful silence.

Another of the Curiatii now came up and began to fight Horatius. But the Roman met the attack with great coolness and skill, and soon killed the second Latin. Thus, under the pretence of running away, Horatius separated the Curiatii and slew two of them. Then he advanced in a furious manner on the other Latin and began a desperate fight with him. Soon he struck him down with a deadly blow. Rome was victorious! From the whole Roman army now came the cry, as if from one man:

"Hail to the brave Horatius! Hail to the champion and savior of his country!"

Then they seized Horatius in their arms and bore him in triumph to King Tullus, who placed on his head the laurel wreath of victory. This was one of the ways by which the Romans honored any of their soldiers who had been very brave in battle. But they also honored Horatius by erecting a statue of him in one of the temples of the city.

III

With songs of joy the army marched back to Rome. Horatius walked by the side of the king. A throng of women came forth from the gates of the city, eager to greet the soldiers and to rejoice with them over the great victory. The sister of Horatius was in the throng. She had been secretly engaged to be married to one of the Curiatii, for the Romans and Albans were near neighbors and frequently visited one another in times of peace. When she learned that her brother had slain her lover she began to weep bitterly. Then pointing at Horatius she cried out:

"You have killed my lover. Do not come near me. I hate and curse you."

Horatius, in a fit of anger, suddenly drew his sword and stabbed her to the heart. As she fell dead at his feet he cried in a loud voice:

"So perish the Roman maiden who weeps for her country's enemy!"

For this shocking murder Horatius was tried and sentenced to death. But the people would not allow the sentence to be carried out. He was made to do a certain penance for the crime and afterwards was set free.

THE TARQUINS

I

The next king of Rome was Ancus Mar'ci-us. He was a grandson of Numa Pompilius, and a very good king. He thought that it would be an advantage to Rome to have a sea harbor for ships. So he founded a city at one of the mouths of the Tiber, on the coast of the Mediterranean, about fifteen miles from Rome. The city was called Ostia, which is a Latin word meaning *mouths*. Latin was the language spoken by the Roman people.

During the reign of Ancus Marcius, a rich man named Lu'cu-mo came to live in Rome. He came from Tar-quin'i-i, a town some miles distant from Rome, in a district or country called E-tru'ri-a, so the Romans called him Tar-quin'i-us, which in English is Tarquin.

A very wonderful thing happened to Tarquin while he was on his way to Rome. He drove in a chariot, with his wife Tan'a-quil seated beside him, and their servants following behind. As they were approaching the city an eagle which appeared in the sky above them came gently down and snatched the cap from Tarquin's head with its beak. After hovering around for a few moments the eagle replaced the cap and with loud screams flew away.

Tarquin was much surprised at this strange event. He did not know what to think of it. But Tanaquil was much pleased. She said to her husband that it was a sign sent by the gods and meant that he was to be a great man—perhaps a king.

19

Tarquin was not long in Rome before he became a favorite with everybody. The people liked him because he spent a great deal of money in doing good. The king also liked him and often asked his advice in affairs of government, for Tarquin was a man of great knowledge and wisdom. And when King Ancus became old and felt that his death was near, he appointed Tarquin the guardian of his two sons who were then but boys.

Soon afterwards Ancus died, and the people elected Tarquin king. He reigned for nearly forty years and did a great deal for the good of the city.

II

It was King Tarquin who began the building of the famous temple of Jupiter on the Saturnian Hill—the same hill on which stood the fortress that Romulus built. While the workmen were digging for the foundations of the temple they found a man's head so well preserved that it looked as if it had been buried quite recently. This was so strange a thing that the augurs were asked about it, and they said it was a sign that Rome would become the *head* or chief city of the world. So the new building was called the Capitol, from *caput*, the Latin word for *head*, and the hill was called the Cap'it-o-line Hill. This has given our language a word. We call the building in which our Congress meets—as well as that in which a state legislature meets—the Capitol.

It took a long time to finish the Capitol, but when finished it was a great and beautiful building. It covered more than eight acres. Its gates or doors were of solid brass, thickly plated with gold. The walls inside were all marble, ornamented with beautiful figures engraved in silver.

Tarquin also began several other works in Rome, which were too great and costly to be finished in a lifetime. One of them was a wall round the city. The wall that Romulus made was only round Palatine Hill. But since then the city had been much enlarged. In course of time it covered seven hills. This is why Rome is often called the seven-hilled city. The seven hills were the Palatine, the Capitoline, the Cæ'li-an, the Quirinal, the Es'qui-line, the Vim'i-nal, and the A'ven-tine.

One of the other things Tarquin did was to establish a kind of police called *lictors*. These were officers who always walked before the king whenever he appeared in public. Each lictor bore upon his shoulder an ax enclosed in a bundle of rods tied with a red strap. This was called the *fas'ces*. It was a mark of the power of the king. The ax meant that the king might order criminals to be behead-ed, and the rods meant that he might punish offenders by flogging.

Another work of Tarquin was the Circus, afterwards called the Circus Max'i-mus (*great circus*). This was a place where horse-races and games and shows of various kinds were held. The Romans were very fond of such amuse-ments. Great numbers of them always went to the shows, but it was easy for them to go, for they did not have to pay for admission. The cost of the shows was paid often by rich Romans who wanted to gain the favor of the people, and often by the government.

The circus had no roof, but there were a great many seats all round and in the middle was a large open space for the performers. This space was covered with sand, and was called the *arena*, a word which is Latin for *sand*.

As so many people attended the circus it had to be very large. In the time when Rome was an Empire, about which you will read later on in this book, the Circus Maximus was so large that it contained seats for 250,000 people. From the circus and arena of the Romans these words have come into use in our own language.

III

Besides building a circus, King Tarquin also greatly improved the Forum by making covered walks or porticoes all round it. The Forum was a large open space at the foot of the Capitoline Hill, where public meetings were held, and where people came to hear the news or talk about politics. It was also used as a market-place, and merchants showed their goods in shops or stores along the porticoes. In course of time great buildings were erected round the Forum. There were courts of justice and temples and statues and monuments of various kinds. The Senate House, where the Senate held its meetings, was also in the Forum. From the end of the Forum next the Capitoline Hill there was a passage leading up to the Capitol.

But the most useful thing King Tarquin did was the building of a great sewer through the city and into the Tiber. Before his time there were no sewers in Rome, though the places between the hills were swampy and wet. This made many parts of the city very unhealthy. Tarquin's sewer drained the swamps and carried the water into the river. It crossed the entire city. It was so high and wide that men could sail into it in boats, and it was so strongly built that it has lasted to the present time. The great sewer is still in use.

Tarquin wanted very much to change one of the laws about the army, but an augur named At'ti-us Na'vi-us told him such a thing could not be done without a sign from the gods. This made the king angry, and he thought he would try to show that the augurs had not the power or knowledge they were supposed to have, so he said to Attius:

"Come, now, I will give you a question. I am thinking whether a certain thing I have in my mind can be done or not. Go and find out from your signs if it can be done."

Navius went away, and shortly afterwards returned and told the king that the thing could be done. Then Tarquin said:

"Well, I was thinking whether or not you could cut this stone in two with this razor. As you say it can be done, do it."

Navius took the razor and immediately cut the stone in two with the greatest ease. The king never again doubted the power of the augurs.

IV

On the death of Tarquin his son-in-law Ser'vi-us Tul'li-us was made king. Tarquin had two young sons, and the sons of Ancus Marcius were also living; but the people preferred to have Servius Tullius for their king.

Servius was a very good king. He had many good laws made and, like King Numa Pompilius, he divided some of the public lands among the poor people of the city.

One of the important things Servius did was to finish the wall round the city which Tarquin had begun. This wall was very high. It was made of stone and earth, and on the outside there was a ditch a hundred feet wide and thirty feet deep. There were several gates in the wall, but they were all well guarded night and day by soldiers, so that no enemy could enter.

King Servius was the first to have a census taken in Rome. He made a rule or law that once every five years all the people should assemble in the Campus Martius to be counted. The word *census* is a Latin word, meaning a *counting* or reckoning, and so we use it in our own country for the counting of the people which takes place every ten years.

Servius Tullius was killed by King Tarquin's son, who was also called Tarquin but got the name of Superbus, or Proud, because he was a very haughty and cruel man. The dead body of Servius was left lying on the street where he had been killed, and Tullia, wife of the wicked Tarquin and daughter of the murdered king, drove her chariot over it.

Tarquin the Proud now became king. It was during his reign that the Sib'yl-line Books were brought to Rome. These books were not like our books. They were merely three bundles of loose pieces of parchment, having moral sentences on them written in the Greek language. This is the story of how the books were obtained:

One morning an old woman came to King Tarquin, carrying nine books in her hands. She offered to sell them to the king, but when she named a large sum as the price he laughed at her and ordered her away. The next day the woman came again, but with only six books. She had burned the other three. She offered to sell the six, but she asked the same price that she had asked the day before for the whole nine. The king again laughed at her and drove her away.

The same day Tarquin went to visit the augurs in their temple, and he told them about the old woman and her books. The augurs declared that she was certainly a sibyl and that her books doubtless contained important predictions about Rome.

The sibyls were women who pretended to be able to foretell events. There were sibyls in many countries, but the most famous of them all was the Sibyl of Cu'mæ, a town in the south of Italy. This was the sibyl who brought the books to Tarquin.

Tarquin was now sorry he had not taken the books, and he hoped the woman would come again. She did come on the following day, but she had only three books instead of six. She had burned the other three the day before. The king was very glad to see her, and he bought the remaining three books, but he had to pay just as much for them as the old woman had asked at first for the nine. Then the sibyl disappeared, and was never seen again.

The ordinary books the Romans had were not like the Sibylline Books. They had no printed books, for printing was not known for many centuries after. Their books were written with pens made of reeds. Their paper was made of the pith of a plant called the *papyrus*, and from this name the word *paper* is derived. To make a book they cut the paper into leaves or pages, and after writing on them they pasted the pages one to another sidewise until all the pages of one book were put together. This long strip was made into a cylindrical roll, and was called a *volume*, from the Latin word *volumen*, a roll. When the volume was being read it was held in both hands, the reader unrolling it with one hand and rolling it with the other.

The Sibylline Books were put in the temple of Jupiter on the Capitoline Hill. Two officers were appointed to keep watch over them. Whenever the Romans were going to war, or had any serious trouble, they would consult the books. The way they did it was this: one of the officers would open the stone chest where the books were kept and take out the first piece of parchment he laid his hand on. Then the Greek sentence found on the piece would be translated into Latin. It was sometimes very hard to tell what the sentence really meant. Often they had to guess. When they made sense out of it they said that it was a prophecy of the sibyl and would surely come to pass.

JUNIUS BRUTUS

I

Tarquin the Proud had a nephew named Junius Brutus. He seemed to be a simpleton, but he was really a very wise man. His brother had been murdered by the king, and he feared the same fate himself, so he pretended to be half-witted and went about saying and doing silly things. Tarquin therefore did him no harm, but rather pitied him.

Two sons of Tarquin once went to a noted fortune-teller, taking Brutus with them. The young men asked several questions. One was:

"Who shall rule Rome after Tarquin?"

The fortune-teller gave this answer:

"Young men, whichever of you shall first kiss your mother shall be the next ruler of Rome."

The king's sons at once started for home, each eager to be the first to kiss his mother. But Brutus thought that something else was really meant by the answer. So after they had left the fortune-teller he managed to stumble and fall on his face. Then he kissed the ground, saying, "The earth is the true mother of us all." And as we shall see, Brutus became the next ruler of Rome.

II

The eldest son of Tarquin was named Sextus. He was a very bad man. He deeply injured a beautiful woman named Lu-cre'ti-a, the wife of Col-la-ti'nus, his cousin.

26

Lucretia told her husband and father and Junius Brutus of what Sextus had done and called upon them to punish him for his wicked deed. Then she plunged a dagger into her breast and fell dead. Brutus drew the dagger from her bleeding body and, holding it up before his horrified companions, exclaimed:

"I vow before the gods to avenge the wronged Lucretia. Not one of the Tarquins shall ever again be king in Rome. Rome shall have no more kings."

They all vowed with Brutus that Lucretia should be avenged and that there should be no more kings in Rome. Then they took up her body and carried it to the Forum. There they showed it to the people, who gathered around in horror at the sight. Brutus no longer appeared dull and simple, but stood with head erect and flashing eyes and spoke to the crowd in eloquent, stirring words.

"See what has come from the evil deeds of the Tarquins!" he shouted, pointing to the dead woman. "Let us free ourselves from the rule of these wicked men. Down with Tarquin the tyrant! No more kings in Rome!"

The people were much excited by his speech, and they made the Forum ring with their cries:

"Down with Tarquin! Down with Tarquin! No more kings! No more kings!"

Then they resolved to take the power of king away from Tarquin and to banish him and his family from Rome. They also decided to adopt the good laws which had been made years before by King Servius Tullius, and to choose two men each year to govern the nation, instead of a king. The men were to be called consuls and were to rule in turn—one for one month, the other for the next, and so on for twelve months. At the end of the year two new consuls were to be elected.

Meanwhile news of the revolt reached King Tarquin, who was at the time in camp with his army some distance from Rome. He instantly mounted his horse and rode in haste to the city. When he reached the gates he found them shut against him. As he stood impatiently demanding to be admitted, a Roman officer appeared on the wall and told him of the sentence of banishment. Tarquin rode away, and Rome was rid of him forever (510 B.C.).

III

The people elected Junius Brutus and Lucius Collatinus, the husband of Lucretia, to be their first consuls; but after a short time Collatinus resigned, because he was himself a Tarquin. Pub'li-us Va-le'ri-us was elected in his stead.

Tarquin now sent messengers for his household goods and other things belonging to him which were in Rome. The messengers while in the city had secret meetings with a number of young men of noble families, and a plot was formed to restore Tarquin to the throne.

The young nobles vowed that they would destroy the new republic and bring back the king, for they did not like government by the common people. But while they were making their plans an intelligent slave overheard what they were saying. This slave went to Brutus and told him of the plot. All engaged in it were at once arrested and put in prison. Two sons of Brutus himself, Titus and Ti-be'ri-us, were found among the plotters.

When Brutus learned that his own children were traitors he was overcome with sorrow. For several days he shut himself up in his house and would see no one. But when the day for the trial came he did his duty sternly as judge—the consuls being judges as well as rulers. Titus and Tiberius were proved guilty of treason, together with the others, and Brutus sentenced them to be whipped with rods and then beheaded. He even was a witness of the execution of the sentence, and we are told that he sat unmoved in his chair and did not turn away his eyes while his two sons were put to death. It was his duty to punish traitors, and he did his duty without sparing his own flesh and blood.

After the loss of his sons Brutus became dull and melancholy and appeared to care very little for life.

Tarquin made an attempt to take Rome, with the aid of the people of two cities of Etruria, and Brutus led the Romans to the field to fight against their former king. During the first part of the battle, a son of Tarquin rode furiously at Brutus to kill him. Brutus saw him and advanced rapidly on his horse to meet the attack. When they came together each ran his spear through the body of the other, and both were killed.

The death of Brutus maddened the Romans, and they fought fiercely until dark. Then the armies went to their camps, and no one knew which side had won. But in the middle of the night a loud voice came from a wood close by the camp of the Etruscans, as the people of Etruria were called. The voice said:

"One man more has fallen on the side of the Etruscans than on the side of the Romans; the Romans will conquer in this war."

The Etruscans believed that this was the voice of the god Jupiter, and they were so frightened that they broke up their camp and quickly marched back to their own land.

HORATIUS

For a time Rome was ruled by Publius Valerius. He was a good man. He caused laws to be passed for the benefit of the people and was therefore called Pub-lic'o-la, which means the people's friend. He had to fight Tarquin frequently. The banished king was constantly trying to capture Rome and get back his throne. He got help from various nations and fought very hard, but was never successful in his efforts. At one time he was aided by Lars Por'se-na, king of Clu'si-um, a city of Etruria, who gathered a large army and set out to attack Rome.

But Porsena could not enter the city without crossing the Tiber, and there was only one bridge. This was called the Sublician Bridge. It was so called from the Latin word *sublicæ*, which means wooden beams. When the Romans saw the great army of Etruscans in the distance, they were much alarmed. They were not prepared to fight so powerful a force. The consul thought for a while, and then he resolved to cut down the bridge as the only means of saving Rome. So a number of men were at once set to work with axes and hammers.

It was hard work, for the bridge was very strongly built. Before the beams supporting it were all cut away the army of Porsena was seen approaching the river. What was to be done? It would take a few minutes more to finish the work, and if the farther end of the bridge could be held against the Etruscans for those few minutes all would be well for Rome. But how was it to be held, and who would hold it? Suddenly from the ranks of the Roman soldiers the brave Ho-ra'ti-us Co'cles stepped out and cried to the consul:

"Give me two good men to help me, and I will hold the bridge and stop the enemy from coming over."

Immediately two brave men, Spu'ri-us Lar'ti-us and Titus Her-min'i-us, ran to his side. Then the three hurried over to the other end of the bridge, and stood ready to keep off the enemy.

When the army of Etruscans saw the three men standing to keep them back a shout of laughter went up among them. Three men to keep back thousands! How ridiculous! There the three brave Romans stood, however, at the entrance of the bridge, with determined faces and fearless eyes.

Very quickly three Etruscans—stout, able fighters— came forth from the army to give battle to the three Romans. After a sharp combat the Etruscans were killed. Three more came out and continued the fight, but they too were beaten by Horatius and his companions.

But now the bridge began to shake and crack. Horatius felt that it was about to fall, and he cried to Spurius and Titus to run back to the other side. While they did so he stood alone and defied the whole Etruscan army, which was now rushing upon him. A whole army against one man! Javelins were hurled at him, but he skillfully warded them off with his shield.

Just as the Etruscans reached him the last beam was cut away, and the bridge fell with a tremendous crash. As it was falling Horatius plunged into the Tiber, and praying to the gods for help, he swam to the other side in safety. The Romans received him with shouts of joy, and even the Etruscans could not help raising a cheer in admiration of his bravery.

The three Romans were well rewarded. A fine statue of Horatius was built in one of the squares of the city. On the base of the statue was placed a brass tablet, with an account of the heroic deed engraved on it. The Senate also gave Horatius as much land as he could plow around in a day.

MUCIUS THE LEFT-HANDED

But Porsena still remained with his army on the other side of the river. He thought that by preventing food from being sent into the city he could force the inhabitants to surrender. So he got ships and stationed them on the Tiber to drive away or seize any vessels that should attempt to come to Rome with food.

Now there was in Rome at this time a very brave young man named Ca'i-us Mu'ci-us, and he thought of a plan to save the city. His plan was to march boldly into the enemy's camp and kill King Porsena. So he concealed a sword under his tunic and went across the river to the Etruscan camp. Then he made his way to the place where the king was sitting.

It happened that it was pay day in the army and the soldiers were getting their money. A secretary, who sat beside the king and was dressed very much like him, was talking to the men and giving them orders. Mucius mistook the secretary for Porsena and rushed forward and stabbed him to death. Instantly the daring Roman was seized by the guards. He heard the soldiers crying out that the secretary was killed. Then he knew what a mistake he had made.

Porsena was greatly enraged at seeing his secretary killed, and in a loud and angry voice he commanded Mucius to tell who he was and why he had committed such a deed. Without showing any sign of fear the bold Mucius answered:

"I am a Roman citizen. I came here to kill you, because you are an enemy of my country. I have failed, but there are others to come after me who will not fail. Your life will be constantly in danger, and you will be killed when you least expect it."

On hearing these words Porsena jumped from his seat in a great fury and threatened to burn Mucius to death if he did not at once tell all about the others who were coming to kill him. But Mucius was not frightened, and to show how little he cared about the king's threat he thrust his right hand into the flame of a fire which had been lighted close by and held it there without flinching. At the same time he cried out to the king:

"Behold how little we Romans care for pain when it is to defend our country."

Porsena was astonished at this sight, and he so much admired the courage and patriotism of the Roman that he ordered the guards to set him free. Then Mucius said to the king:

"In return for your kindness I now tell you of my own free will what I would not tell you when you threatened me with punishment. Know then that three hundred Roman youths have bound themselves by oath to kill you, each to make the attempt in his turn. The lot fell first on me. I have failed, but the attempt will be made again and again until some one succeeds."

King Porsena was so terrified on hearing this that he resolved to make peace at once with Rome. So he immediately sent messengers to the Senate, and terms of peace were quickly agreed upon.

The Senate rewarded Mucius by giving him a tract of land on the banks of the Tiber. This land was afterwards called the Mucian Meadows. Mucius himself got the name of Sçæv'o-la, a Latin word which means *left-handed*. He had lost the use of his right hand by burning it in the fire.

CORIOLANUS

I

One of the great men of Rome not long after the banishment of the Tarquins was Caius Marcius. He was a member of a noble family, and from his youth he had been noted for his bravery.

In his time there was a war between the Romans and the Vol'sci-ans, a people of a district in Latium. The Romans made an attack on Co-ri'o-li, the capital city of the Volscians, but were defeated and driven back. Caius Marcius reproached the Roman soldiers for running from the enemy. His words made them ashamed and they turned again to the fight. With Caius at their head they sent the Volscians flying back into the city. Caius followed the enemy to the gates, which were partly open. When he saw this he shouted to the Romans:

"The gates are open for us; let us not be afraid to enter!"

Caius himself sprang in and kept the gates open for the Romans. After a short fight the city was taken.

Then everybody said that it was Caius who had taken Corioli, and that he should be called after the name of the city he had won. So ever afterwards he was known as Co'ri-o-la'nus.

II

But though Coriolanus was a brave soldier and always ready to fight for Rome, he had some qualities that were

not so good. He had great contempt for the common people, and he took part with those who tried to oppress
them.

Only a little while before the taking of Corioli, there was
a serious trouble between the people and the patricians.
A great many of the people earned their living by farming.
But when there was a war the strong men had to become
soldiers, and as Rome was almost constantly at war the
men were nearly always away from their farms. Very
often, therefore, they had to borrow money to support
their families while they themselves were away fighting,
for at this time Roman soldiers got no regular pay.

Now it was the rich patricians who loaned the money,
and if it was not paid back at the time agreed upon they
could put the people who owed it in jail, or they could sell
their wives and children as slaves.

In this way the plebeians often suffered much hardship.
At last a great number of them resolved to leave Rome
and make a settlement for themselves somewhere else in
Italy. The patricians did not like this very much, for if the
common people went away there would be a scarcity of
soldiers for the army. So the Senate, after thinking the
matter over, proposed that the plebeians should elect officers of their own, to be called trib'unes, who should have
power to veto laws they did not like, that is, prevent them
from being passed. The word *veto*, which is Latin for *I for-
bid*, is used in the same way in our own country. The
President of the United States and the governors of some
states have, within certain limits, power to prevent the
passing of laws they do not approve. This is called the
veto power.

The plebeians were pleased with the proposal that they
were to have tribunes, so they returned to Rome, and for
a time there was peace between them and the patricians.

But Coriolanus and other patricians were opposed to
the election of tribunes, because they thought it gave the
common people too much power. Once when there was a
famine in Rome, and the poor were suffering greatly from

want of food, the Greeks living in Sicily sent several ships laden with corn to Rome to relieve the people in distress. When the corn arrived the Senate was about to order that it should be divided among the people who needed it, but Coriolanus interfered.

"No, no," he said, "if the people want corn let them first give up their tribunes. It must be either no corn or no tribunes."

The people were so angry when they heard of this speech that they talked about killing Coriolanus. And they would have done so but for the wise advice of the tribunes.

"No, no," said the tribunes, "you must not kill him; that would be against the law. But you can have him tried for treason against the people and we will be his accusers."

Coriolanus was then ordered to appear before the assembly of the people to be tried, for the people had power to try in their assemblies persons charged with such offences. But Coriolanus was afraid the assembly would condemn him, so he secretly fled from the city, leaving his family behind, and went to a town of the Volscians.

The chief of the Volscians received Coriolanus in a friendly manner. Coriolanus then told him why he had left Rome. The Volscian chief was glad to hear it. He had long wanted to fight the Romans, but had been afraid to make the attempt. With the aid of such a soldier as Coriolanus, however, he was sure that Rome might be taken. So he raised a large army and put it under the command of the great Roman.

III

The Volscian army, led by Coriolanus, captured many cities belonging to the Roman Republic. At last Coriolanus resolved to attack Rome itself, and he marched his army towards the city. The Romans just then were not very well prepared for a battle, so the Senate decided to send messengers to Coriolanus to beg him to spare his native city and make terms of peace.

The messengers chosen were five of the leading nobles, and they at once set out for the Volscian camp. Coriolanus received them cordially, for they were old friends; but he said that he would not spare Rome unless the Romans would give up all the lands and cities which they had taken from the Volscians in former wars.

To this the Senate would not agree, and Coriolanus refused to listen to any other terms. The Romans then began to prepare for battle, though they feared very much that they would be defeated.

But while the men were thus in fear and doubt, the women of Rome saved the city! Va-le'ri-a, a noble Roman lady, remembered that Coriolanus had always dearly loved his mother.

"Perhaps," thought she, "he may listen to her though he will hear no one else."

So Valeria, with a large number of noble ladies, went to the house of Ve-tu'ri-a, the mother of Coriolanus, and said to her:

"The gods have put it into our hearts to come and ask you to join with us to save our country from ruin. Come then with us to the camp of your son and pray him to show mercy."

The aged mother at once agreed to go, so she got ready immediately and set out for the camp of the Volscians, accompanied by a great number of ladies and her son's wife and little children. It was a strange sight, this long line of Roman ladies, all dressed in mourning, and even the Volscian soldiers showed them respect as they passed along.

Coriolanus happened to be sitting in front of his tent in the Volscian camp with a number of officers around him as the procession came in view. "Who are these women?" he asked. Before an answer could be given he saw that among them were his mother and wife and children, and he stood up and hastened forward to meet them. They fell on their knees and begged him to spare his native city.

Coriolanus seemed deeply distressed. He made no answer, but bent his head, pressed his hand to his breast and gazed down upon the dear ones who knelt at his feet. Then his mother said:

"If I had no son Rome would not be in this danger. I am too old to bear much longer your shame and my own misery. Look to your wife and children; if you continue in your present course you will send them to an early death."

Coriolanus was so grieved that for some minutes he could not speak. At last he cried out:

"Oh, mother, what have you done to me? You have saved Rome, but you have ruined your son."

Then he embraced his mother and looked at her sadly for a moment. He also embraced and kissed his wife and children and told them to go back to Rome, for they would be safe there. The women then returned to the city and Coriolanus marched away with the Volscian army. Rome was saved!

Coriolanus lived the rest of his life with the Volscians, but he never again made war against his native city. It is supposed that he died about the middle of the fifth century before Christ.

THE FABII

At about the time in which Coriolanus lived the family of the Fa'bi-i were very powerful in Rome. Among the leaders or chief men of the family at that period were Quin'tus Fa'bi-us, Marcus Fabius, and Cæ'so Fabius.

In those times the Roman nobles were very rich and powerful. They held all the high offices of government and cared very little about the welfare of the plebeians. Often they treated them very harshly.

The Fabii also treated the plebeians harshly. Once when Quintus Fabius defeated the Volscians in a battle, he sold all the valuable things he took from the enemy and put the money into the public treasury. Such things were called spoils. The Roman generals usually divided the spoils among the soldiers. This was the way the soldiers were paid in those days. But Quintus Fabius would not divide the spoils. So the soldiers were very bitter against him.

But some time afterwards Marcus Fabius was elected consul, and once after a great battle with the Ve'i-en-ti-ans, a people of Etruria, he took the entire care of the poor wounded soldiers and supplied all their wants at his own expense.

The next year his brother Cæso Fabius was consul, and he tried to get the Senate to divide among the poor citizens the lands that had been taken from the Veientians and other people whom the Romans had defeated in war. Often afterwards in the Senate the voice of a Fabius was heard speaking for justice to the plebeians. The common people, therefore, soon loved the whole family of the Fabii instead of hating them as they had before.

The nobles were very angry because the Fabii took the side of the plebeians, and they threatened to do all they could against them. Now the Fabii saw clearly that it would be useless to attempt to fight the nobles, because the nobles had a great deal of power and could do almost whatever they pleased in Rome. Therefore, the Fabii thought that it would be better for them to remove from the city and make a new home for themselves somewhere else. So they resolved to do this, and the place they selected was on the banks of the River Crem'e-ra, a few miles from Rome.

At this time the Romans were again at war with the Veientians. These people lived in Ve'i-i, a city on the Cremera River. One day, when there was a discussion in the Roman Senate about this war, Cæso Fabius said:

"As you know, we of the house of the Fabii are going to leave Rome and settle on the borders of the country of the Veientians. If you give us permission we will fight those people and try to defeat them for the honor of Rome and the glory of our house. We will ask neither money nor men from the Senate. We will carry on the war with our own men and at our own cost."

The senators were glad of the chance to get rid of the Fabii, and so they at once gave them the permission they asked for. The Fabii then began to make preparations for their departure. There were over three hundred men in addition to women-folk, children, and servants, and when all were ready they marched out of the city to their new home with Cæso Fabius at their head.

At first the Fabii had only a camp on the Cremera River, but afterwards they built a small city, with a strong fortress. Many good Roman soldiers came and joined them, and soon they had a fine army of earnest, devoted men.

The Veientians were soon conquered. Fabius and his brave men defeated them in several battles, and at last the Veientians made up their minds that they had got enough of war. Then they returned to their own city of Veii and remained quiet for a long time. But they declared that they would destroy the Fabii whenever they could get the chance.

Now it was an old custom of the Fabii to have a special worship of the gods on a certain day of every year. Early in the morning of that day all the men of the family would go in a body to a famous temple on a hill near Rome and have religious services for several hours. The men took no arms with them, as it was thought improper to go armed to religious worship.

The Veientians heard of this annual religious service of the Fabii and saw in it a chance for revenge. So they resolved to kill the Fabii the next time they went to the temple for their special service. When the day came the Fabii set out as usual. On their way to the temple they had to go over a road which had high, steep rocks on each side. There a large number of Veientian soldiers hid themselves, and when the unsuspecting Fabii came along a furious attack was made on them from front and rear. Without arms they could not fight very well. They made the best defence they could, but it was useless. They were all killed except one young man who escaped to Rome. Thus the cowardly Veientians had their revenge.

CINCINNATUS

I

In the mountains east of Latium there lived a rather wild people called Æ'qui-ans, who were very often at war with Rome. After some time of peace and good conduct these people suddenly began to plunder the rich farms of the Romans. This was about four hundred and fifty years before the birth of Christ and not long after the Veientians had destroyed the Fabian family. As soon as the Roman Senate heard what the Æquians were doing it sent messengers to the Æquian king to complain of the wrong. The messengers found the king in his camp, sitting near a huge oak tree. But when they spoke to him he answered them rudely, saying:

"I am too busy now with other matters. Go tell your message to the oak yonder!"

This made the messengers very angry, and one of the them said:

"We shall tell it to the oak, but we shall tell it also to the gods and call them to witness how you have broken the peace! And they shall be on our side when we come to punish you and your people for the crimes you have committed against us."

And it is said that the angry messengers did tell the message to the oak, and to all the other trees around, and boldly shouted that war would come from this insult to Rome.

Then the messengers returned to Rome and told the

Senate how they had been insulted by the Æquian king. The Senate at once declared war against the Æquians and ordered the Consul Minu'ci-us to lead an army against them.

The Romans easily won a few battles at first. Then the Æquians began to retreat as if they did not mean to fight any more. The Romans followed swiftly, until they were drawn into a narrow valley on each side of which were high, rocky hills. It was a trap, and the Romans knew it before they had marched very far from the entrance.

The Æquian king then closed up the valley with strong barricades and placed his troops at the entrance and along the hills, so that the Romans could not get out.

In the valley there was very little grass for the horses and no food for the men, so that if the Romans were not soon relieved both they and their horses would die of hunger.

II

But luckily for the Romans a few of their horsemen had managed to get out of the valley before the Æquians closed it. These horsemen rode as fast as they could to Rome and told the Senate how Minucius and his soldiers were placed. What was to be done? No one seemed to know at first, but after a good deal of discussion, a senator said:

"Let us make Lucius Quinc'ti-us dictator. He is the only man who can save us."

The Senate agreed to this, and so Lucius Quinctius was chosen dictator. A dictator had more power than the Senate or the consuls. All his commands had to be obeyed just as if he were a king. But there was not a dictator always. A dictator was appointed only when there was some great danger, and he held office only for six months.

Lucius Quinctius belonged to a noble family. He was a great soldier and had won many battles for his country. He had such beautiful, long, curly hair that the people called him *Cin'cin-na'tus,* which means *curly-haired,* and this is the name by which he is known in history.

At the time Cincinnatus was appointed dictator he lived on a small farm outside of Rome. He worked on the farm himself, and when the messengers from the Senate came to tell him that he had been chosen dictator they found him ploughing in one of his fields. He left his plough where it stood and hastened to Rome, where he was welcomed by all the people.

The first thing he did was to raise a new army. He gave orders that every man of suitable age should buckle on his sword and be ready in a few hours to march to the help of Minucius and his soldiers.

Before evening Cincinnatus and his army marched out of the city for the Alban Hills, where the Romans were shut up. They reached the place in the early morning and formed in a line all around the hills. The Æquians then found themselves hemmed in on every side between two Roman armies—the army of Minucius and the army of Cincinnatus. They fought as well as they could, but they were quickly overpowered, so that they could do nothing but cry to the Roman commander to spare their lives.

Cincinnatus spared their lives, but he made them *pass under the yoke.* The yoke was formed of two spears, fixed upright in the ground, and a third fastened across near the top from one to the other. Cincinnatus made the Æquians lay down their arms and pass out, every man of them, under the yoke of spears. They had to bend their heads as they did so, for the spears were not very long, and the one on the top was only a few feet from the ground. The yoke was set up between two lines of Roman soldiers, and as the Æquians passed under it the Romans jeered at them and taunted them.

Having to pass under the yoke was regarded as the greatest disgrace that could happen to soldiers. Many much preferred to suffer death. The practice has given to our language the word *subjugate*, meaning to subdue or conquer, from the Latin words *sub*, under, and *jugum*, a yoke.

When the soldiers of Consul Minucius came out of the valley they shouted for joy and crowded around Cincinnatus, thanking him as their deliverer and protector. "Let us give Cincinnatus a golden crown!" they cried; but the great general only smiled, shook his head, and gave the order for the homeward march.

Great was the rejoicing in Rome when the news of the victory was received. The Senate ordered that there should be a general holiday and a grand parade through the city. And so the victorious army marched into Rome amid the shouts and cheers of the people.

Cincinnatus rode in a splendid chariot drawn by six handsome black horses. He wore the dress of dictator of Rome, and on his head was a laurel wreath. Behind his chariot the Æquian king and his chiefs walked, looking very humble and forlorn. Following them were slaves laden with the arms and other valuable things taken from the enemy's camp. With bugles and trumpets gayly sounding, the parade went through the city. The chariot of Cincinnatus was followed by a throng of people cheering and crying, "Hail to the Dictator! Hail to the Conqueror!" Flowers were showered upon him and thrown before his chariot wheels.

A few days afterward Cincinnatus gave up the office of dictator and went back to his little farm.

CAMILLUS

I

About three hundred and eighty years before the birth of Christ the Romans had another war with the Veientians. During this war they tried to take the rich city of Veii, which was about twelve miles from Rome. But there was a great wall of stone all around the city, and the gates, which were of brass, were very high and very strong. So the Romans, though they tried as hard as they could for seven years, were not able to take Veii.

And to make matters worse for them it was reported that twelve Etruscan cities were going to send armies to help the Veientians. It was also said that as soon as the twelve armies had driven the Romans away from the walls of Veii, they would march to Rome and destroy the city.

The Romans were much alarmed by these reports, and they resolved that there should be a dictator. So the Senate appointed a dictator, and the man appointed was Marcus Fu'ri-us Ca-mil'lus.

Camillus was one of the greatest men of Rome. He belonged to a very rich and powerful family, and he was a great soldier. When he was made dictator he raised a large army and marched at once to Veii. He tried a long time to break down the walls or gates, but he could not do it. Then he thought of the plan of digging a tunnel under the walls.

This seemed a good idea, so Camillus set a great number of his men to work. Soon they had a tunnel dug under the walls and so far under the city that they thought they were as far as the great temple of Juno, which was in the fort or strongest part of Veii. Here they stopped to consider what next to do. Suddenly the sound of voices, as of people talking in the temple above them, reached their ears. So they sent for Camillus, and when he came he listened to the voices.

Now it happened that at that moment the king of Veii was in the temple preparing to offer an ox as a sacrifice to Juno and praying to the goddess to save the city from the Romans. The ox was killed and its carcass was ready to be laid on the altar. After the king had prayed one of the priests, pretending that he had received an answer from Juno, cried out:

"The goddess declares she will give victory to him who offers this as a sacrifice upon the altar."

As soon as Camillus, who was listening all the time, heard these words of the priest, he ordered his men to break an opening in the earth over their heads. This was quickly done, and the Romans sprang through into the midst of the worshipers. They at once seized the carcass of the ox, and Camillus himself offered it upon the altar to Juno. Then he and his companions rushed out of the temple and opened the gates of the city before the astonished and frightened people knew what was being done.

As soon as the gates were opened the Roman soldiers poured in by thousands. The Veientians fought bravely, but they were quickly defeated, and their great and rich city was at last in the hands of the Romans.

In those times, as has already been said, it was the custom to divide among the victorious soldiers the valuable things taken from a defeated enemy. The riches of Veii were, therefore, divided among the Roman soldiers, and there were so many precious things—gold and silver and jewelry—that the men were quite rich when each got his share.

II

Some time after the taking of Veii the Romans were at war with the Fa-lis'ci-ans, another people of Etruria, and Camillus went with an army to besiege their chief town, which was called Fa-le'ri-i. He made his camp in front of the walls, stationed soldiers all round and tried hard to take the town. But the Faliscians were very strong and brave, and they defended their town so well that Camillus began to be afraid he would not be able to take it at all.

Now there was at that time in Falerii a schoolmaster who taught the sons of the chief citizens of the town. This schoolmaster used to take his boys every day for a walk outside the walls. One day he led them within the lines of the Roman army and brought them into the camp of Camillus.

Camillus was surprised at seeing the boys. He asked the schoolmaster who they were and why he had brought them there. The schoolmaster told who the boys were and then said:

"I bring them here to give them up to you. In doing this I give you up the city, for their fathers will surrender the city to you in order to get back their children."

Camillus stood for a moment in silence, gazing at the traitor with a look of disgust. Then in an angry voice he cried out:

"Villain, we Romans are not so base as you are. We do not make war upon children, but upon men who do us wrong."

He then ordered some of his soldiers to tie the school-master's hands behind his back and to give each of the boys a rod, telling them to scourge the traitor before them into the city. This the boys did with a hearty good-will. They whipped the unworthy schoolmaster into Falerii, and when the people saw the sight and heard of the noble conduct of Camillus, they resolved not to fight any more against so good a man. So they sent ambassadors to Rome to make peace, and the Romans and Faliscians became good friends.

III

Not long after this time one of the tribunes brought a charge against Camillus that he had kept for his own use more than his fair share of the spoils of Veii. Some valuable things were noticed in his house, and it was said that he had not got them as part of his share. It was believed, therefore, that he had taken them secretly from Veii.

The Romans were very particular upon this point. They had strict laws for the division of spoils obtained in war, and no one was permitted to take more than he was entitled to, according to his rank in the army.

Camillus was summoned to appear in the people's court to answer the charge made against him. But he would not humble himself so much as to go before the plebeians to be tried. He preferred rather to leave Rome forever. So the great Camillus departed from his native city, intending never to return. As he passed out of the gates he prayed to the gods that some dreadful thing might happen to the Romans, so that they would be forced to call him back again to Rome to save the city.

And very soon something did happen which compelled the Romans to ask for the help of Camillus. For a long time a people called the Gauls had been doing a great deal of mischief in some parts of Italy. These people came from the country now known as France, which in ancient times was called Gaul. Thousands of them made their way across the high mountains called the Alps and settled on the plains of northern Italy. For many years they lived in this region. Then they heard that further south the country was very beautiful and was rich in corn and cattle, so they started out in great numbers to conquer it.

They were a strange, savage people, very different from the Romans or the Etruscans. They were very tall and strong and had long, shaggy black hair and dark, fierce faces, so that they appeared very terrible to the Italians. In battle they showed all their savage nature. They rushed furiously at their enemies, yelling at the top of their voices, flourishing enormous swords, and blowing trumpets.

The chief or king of the Gauls at this time was called Bren'nus. He was a man of great strength and size. He wore a golden collar around his neck, and on his arms, which were bare, he sometimes wore bracelets of gold.

The Gauls found the southern lands very much to their liking. They robbed farms, attacked some of the Etruscan cities, and then, after a short time, they marched for Rome. A great Roman army went out to fight them, and the two armies met on the banks of a river called the Al'li-a.

The Roman soldiers had never before seen the dreadful Gauls. They were, therefore, greatly terrified when the tall, fierce-looking savages came running over the plains in vast numbers, shouting furiously and blowing their trumpets. And though the Roman general, Marcus Man'li-us, tried to make his men go forward bravely to meet the Gauls it was useless. They fought badly and were killed by thousands. At last they ran from the field and fled toward Rome.

IV

When the defeated soldiers reached Rome and told what had happened, there was great terror in the city. Most of the people bundled up their household goods and fled to hiding-places in the mountains close by, where they thought they would be safe from the Gauls.

But many of the senators and other brave men, both nobles and plebeians, instead of running away from the city went up to the Capitol, fastened the gates, and made ready for a siege. The Capitol was the most sacred part of the city. It contained splendid statues of Jupiter, Juno, and Minerva, and, as you know, the famous Sibylline Books.

Some old men who had been consuls resolved to remain in the city and wait for the Gauls to come. They thought that if the Gauls should kill them they would then be satisfied and would spare the city. So the patriotic old men dressed themselves in their finest robes and sat in chairs in the Forum, each with an ivory staff in his right hand.

When the Gauls reached the city there was no one to

oppose them. They marched on to the Forum and found the old men, with long white beards, sitting in their chairs, so still that they looked like statues. A Gaul went up to one of them and pulled his beard to see if he were a living person. Instantly the old man raised his staff and struck the barbarian in the face. The Gauls then fell upon the patriots and killed them. Then they began to plunder.

After destroying the greater part of the city the Gauls turned their attention to the Capitol. The rock on which it was built was high and steep.

Brennus led his soldiers up the hill, but the Romans in the Capitol rushed down the narrow road and after a few minutes of brave fighting drove them back. The Gauls made another attempt, but it was no more successful than the first.

Brennus saw that the Romans could not be driven from the Capitol. He therefore decided to starve them out. He put a strong guard at the entrance, so that the Romans could not come out to get food. For weeks the Capitol was thus besieged, but its faithful defenders held out manfully.

Meanwhile the people who had fled from Rome took courage again. They gathered at the city of Veii and organized a strong army to fight the Gauls. But they wanted a commander, and then they thought of Camillus. All agreed that he would be the right man to be their general. So they resolved to send for him, but first they thought they must have the approval of the Senate. Here was a difficulty. How could a messenger get to the Senate while the Gauls were around the Capitol? This puzzled them for a good while, but at last a young man named Pon'ti-us Com-in'i-us volunteered to carry a message to the Capitol.

So on a very dark night Pontius left Veii and swam down the Tiber until he reached the Capitoline Hill. Then he went on shore and crept up the hill as far as the great rock. The Gauls had put no guard there, for they thought no one could climb the rock because it was so steep.

By great efforts Pontius managed to climb up. Several times he was near falling. But by clinging to the vines and bushes that grew on the rock he came to the top at last. His countrymen in the Capitol were delighted to see him. They were also very glad when they heard about the army at Veii, and the Senate at once approved of the proposal about Camillus. It was agreed not only to make him general, but to make him dictator. Then Cominius went down the rock and the hill by the way he had come up and hastened off to Veii.

V

The next day some of the Gauls, while walking along this side of the hill, noticed footmarks in the soil. They also noticed that bushes, growing high up on the rock, were crushed and torn. Then they knew that some one had gone up or come down the cliff, and they resolved to try to go up themselves that night.

So shortly after midnight, when they thought that the Romans would be fast asleep, a party of Gauls began cautiously and silently to clamber up the steep rock. Some placed their shields across their shoulders for others to stand upon, and in this way they supported one another, until at last some of them made their way very near to the top and one got just to the edge of a balcony of the Capitol. No one within the building heard them, not even the watch-dogs.

But at that moment there was a loud cackling of geese. These birds were thought to be favorite birds of the goddess Juno. Many were kept in the Capitol, and some of them happened just then to be at the side the Gauls were climbing up. The movements of the climbers, quiet though they were, disturbed the geese and they began to cackle and flap their wings.

The noise aroused Marcus Manlius from his sleep. He sprang from his bed, seized his sword and shield, and ran to the balcony. There he saw a Gaul climbing on to the parapet and others scrambling up behind. Marcus rushed upon him, struck him in the face with his shield, and tumbled him headlong down the rock.

As the Gaul fell he knocked down some of his companions who were climbing behind him. The geese still kept up their loud cackling, and soon all the Romans were awakened and came quickly to the assistance of Marcus. The Gauls were hurled back as they mounted the rock, and in a few minutes all who had come up were dashed down the steep cliff and killed. Thus the Capitol was saved by the cackling of geese. For his brave action on this occasion Marcus Manlius was honored by being called Marcus *Cap'i-to-li'nus.*

VI

Brennus now saw that he could not take the Capitol, so he thought it would be useless to remain any longer in Rome. He therefore offered to go away if the Senate would give him a thousand pounds of gold. The Senate thought it better to do this. Food was very scarce in the Capitol and in a few days the brave men there would have none at all. They had heard nothing further from the army at Veii and they were not sure that help could come in time to save them.

So the Senate resolved to give the thousand pounds of gold to the Gauls, and an officer named Quin'tus Sul-pit'i-us was sent with some lictors to deliver it to Brennus. But the gold had to be weighed and the Gauls attempted to cheat the Romans by using false weights. When Sulpitius complained of this, Brennus took off his sword and threw it, belt and all, into one of the scales, and when Sulpitius asked what that meant Brennus answered:

"What should it mean but woe to the conquered?"

At that moment Camillus appeared at the gates with his army. He soon learned what was going on. Quickly he marched to the spot and ordered the lictors to take the gold out of the scale and carry it back to the Roman treasury. Then he turned to Brennus and addressing him in a stern voice said:

"We Romans defend our country, not with gold, but with steel."

Immediately there was a battle, and the Gauls were defeated and driven out of the city. Next day there was another battle a few miles from Rome, and the Gauls were again defeated and thousands of them slain.

Camillus then returned to Rome at the head of his victorious army. The people received him with shouts of joy and for several days they had celebrations in his honor. They called him the second Romulus, meaning that he was the second founder of the city. They also called him the FATHER OF HIS COUNTRY.

VII

It was in the time of Camillus that a great hole or chasm, caused perhaps by an earthquake, suddenly appeared in the ground in the middle of the Forum. Workmen were sent to fill it up, but no matter how much earth they threw into it the hole seemed to be as large and deep as before. The Senate then consulted the augurs and they said the hole could not be filled up until what was most valuable in Rome was cast into it. Then the people began to throw in gold and silver and jewelry, but still the hole was as deep as ever. At last a young man named Curtius said that the most valuable things the Romans had were their arms and their courage. Then he put on his armor and his sword and mounting his horse rode into the Forum and leaped into the great hole. Immediately it closed up behind him, and neither he nor his horse was ever seen again.

In the old Roman stories Curtius is much praised as a patriot and hero. The people thought he had saved his country from some great evil, which they believed would have happened to it if the hole in the Forum had not been closed up.

MANLIUS TORQUATUS

Marcus Manlius, who commanded the Roman army at the battle of Allia and who so well defended the Capitol against the Gauls, belonged to a family known as the Man'li-i. This family gave many brave generals to the Republic. One of them was named Titus Manlius.

Some years after the siege of the Capitol Titus had a remarkable fight with a huge Gaul. The Gauls had come back to make war again upon Rome. Their army was encamped near a bridge on the A'ni-o, a small river a few miles from the city, and the Roman army sent to oppose them was on the other side of the river, waiting for a good opportunity for battle.

Every day a Gaul of gigantic size, who wore round his neck a collar or chain of twisted gold threads, used to come to the bridge to insult the Romans. He would call them cowards who were afraid to fight. One day he dared them to send some one out to fight with him. Manlius at once accepted the challenge, and the two immediately took their places in an open space within sight of both armies.

The Gaul was so tall and strong that the Roman appeared like a boy beside him, and everybody thought the big warrior would have an easy victory. But Titus was very quick in his movements. For a few moments after the fight began he skillfully dodged the furious blows of his opponent. Then he suddenly ran close up to him, sprang under his great shield and plunged his sword deep into the Gaul's body.

The Gaul fell to the ground dead. Then Titus took the golden collar from the dead man's neck and put it on his own. So afterwards he was called Manlius Tor-qua'tus, from the word *torques*, which is Latin for a *twisted collar*.

Manlius Torquatus became consul, but he was not much liked by the people, for he was a very stern and severe ruler. During a war which the Romans had with the Latins and some tribes of South Italy, Manlius was in command of the Roman army. He marched to meet the enemy, who were assembled in force at the foot of Mount Vesuvius.

While the two armies were encamped opposite to each other, Manlius ordered that none of his men should fight with any of the Latins until the word for battle was given. Soon after a Latin officer met young Manlius, the consul's son, riding in front of the lines with a troop of his comrades. They entered into conversation about the coming battle, and each boasted of the valor of the soldiers on his own side. At last the Latin officer challenged the young Roman to single combat.

"Wilt thou," he cried, "measure thy strength with mine? It will then be seen how much the Latin horseman excels the Roman."

Manlius accepted the challenge, and in the fight which immediately took place he was the victor. He killed the Latin and, according to the custom of those times, stripped him of his armor and carried it to the Roman camp. Then he went to tell his father what he had done.

"Father," said he, "I present you this armor, which I have taken from the enemy. I hope you will accept it as a proof that I am ready and able to do my duty as a Roman soldier."

Torquatus looked at his son sadly and then said:

"My son, you say you are willing to do your duty as a soldier. But the first duty of a soldier is obedience. This duty you have not performed, for you have just now disobeyed me, your commander. You have fought with the enemy without receiving orders to do so. But you shall not escape punishment because you are my son."

Then turning to his lictors he said:

"Go, bind him to a stake and cut off his head."

At this cruel order loud cries of horror came from the soldiers. Young Manlius threw himself at his father's feet and begged for mercy. But the stern consul turned away from him and ordered the lictors to perform their duty. So the brave young Manlius was led to a stake and bound, and with one stroke of the lictor's axe his head was cut from his body.

Soon afterwards there was a battle between the two armies, and the Romans gained a great victory. But the war continued for some time longer. It ended, however, in the defeat of the Latins. Manlius took possession of one of their towns—the town of An'ti-um, on the Mediterranean coast—and compelled the inhabitants to give up their warships.

War vessels and galleys in those times had sharp prows made for the purpose of running into and breaking through the sides of other vessels. The prow was a beam, with pointed irons fastened to it, and a metal figure resembling the beak or head of a bird or other animal. This beak was called a *rostrum*.

When the Romans captured the warships of Antium they broke off the beaks and carried them to Rome. There they fastened them as ornaments to the platform in the Forum, from which orators addressed the people. Hence the word rostrum came to mean a platform or pulpit for public speaking, and in this sense it is now used in our own language.

APPIUS CLAUDIUS CÆCUS

I

Soon after the defeat of the Gauls there lived in Rome a great man named Ap'pi-us Clau'di-us. He belonged to one of the highest families of the city. He was consul for two years, and for several years he held the office of censor (312–308 B.C.).

The censor was a very high and important officer. He was not only head of the department for taking the census, but he had charge of the collecting of the taxes, the erecting of public buildings, and the making of roads and streets.

Appius Claudius was a great soldier. Every Roman citizen had to be a soldier, and every man who was consul had to be able to lead armies and to fight and win battles. But Appius Claudius was chiefly famous for the great public works he planned and directed in Rome, which at that time was a city with a population of about three hundred thousand. One of these works was an aqueduct which brought water to the city from a lake eight miles distant. The Roman aqueducts were the best in the world. Some of them that were built over two thousand years ago are still in use.

But the greatest work of Appius Claudius was the making of a road from Rome to Cap'u-a, a distance of one hundred and twenty miles. This road was called the Appian Way in honor of Appius. It was also called the "queen of roads" because it was so well built. Parts of it are still in existence. The Romans had good roads as well as good aqueducts. They were the best road-builders in the world.

While he was censor Appius Claudius very much improved Rome. He was called "the greatest of his countrymen in the works of peace." Even after he retired from office he had great influence in public affairs. His advice was asked by both plebeians and nobles.

Once during the first war which the Romans had with the Greeks the advice of Appius was of great benefit to Rome. At that time there were many Greek settlements in the south of Italy. One of the Greek towns was called Ta-ren'tum. It was built close to the sea and had a very good harbor.

Many of the people of this town were well educated. In those days the Greeks were mostly an educated people. They were fond of learning and of art. They called the Romans barbarians and were not friendly to them.

Once when a Roman fleet entered the bay of Tarentum, the people of the town attacked it and after taking five of the ships put the crews to death. When the news of this outrage reached Rome the Senate sent ambassadors to demand satisfaction. One of the ambassadors was a man named Lu'ci-us Pos-thu'mi-us. When they arrived at Tarentum they were met by a noisy crowd of people of the town, who made fun of their dress.

The Romans wore an outer dress called a toga. It was a large white woollen cloth, in the shape of a half circle, four or five yards long and of nearly the same width. In putting on this garment they doubled it lengthwise, then passed one end over the left shoulder and under the opposite arm and again over the left shoulder, the other end reaching nearly to the ground in front. The Tarentines laughed at the toga of the Roman ambassadors. They said it was a dress fit only for savages.

In a short time the ambassadors were taken to the public theatre, where the people had assembled to hear the message from Rome. Posthumius spoke to them in Greek, but as this was not his own language he pronounced many of the words in a peculiar way, and the Tarentines laughed. The Roman went on, however, in a dignified manner and finished his speech as if he had not noticed the insult.

Just then a Tarentine moved forward to the place where Posthumius stood and threw some dirt on his white toga. The ambassador held up the soiled garment with his hand and said that Tarentum would be made to suffer for the outrage. Then the theatre rang with laughter and offensive cries.

"Laugh on," said Posthumius, "you may laugh now but you shall weep hereafter. The stain on this toga shall be washed out in your blood!"

Then the ambassadors left the theatre and at once set out for Rome. When they appeared before the Senate Posthumius showed the stain on his toga as proof of the insult offered to Rome by the Tarentines. The Senate at once declared war on Tarentum and sent a powerful army to attack it.

II

At this time the Tarentines had no general they thought would be able to fight the Romans. So they sent across the sea to E-pi'rus, in Greece, for the king of that country to come and help them. The name of this king was Pyr'rhus. He was a great soldier and commander and was nearly always engaged in war. He consented to help the Tarentines and crossed over to Italy with a great army in which there was a number of fighting elephants.

When Pyrrhus entered Tarentum he made himself master of the city. The Tarentines were very fond of plays and amusements of all kinds. Pyrrhus closed the theatres, stopped all the amusements and made the people drill as soldiers all day long.

As soon as he was ready to fight he marched out with his army of Greeks and Tarentines against the Romans, and there was a great battle near the city of Her'a-cle'a.

Both sides fought well for hours, but the Greeks at last began to fall back. They could not stand against the steady, fierce attacks made by the Romans.

Then Pyrrhus brought his elephants upon the field. He had seventy of them, and they were thoroughly trained to fight. They would run into the ranks of the enemy, knock the soldiers down and trample them to death, or lay hold of them with their trunks and throw them high into the air.

As the elephants stood in line waiting for the order to charge, the Romans looked at them with wonder and fear. They knew nothing about elephants, for they had never seen any before. And when the huge beasts came charging furiously across the field, making strange noises, many of the Roman soldiers were terribly frightened and began to run away. The elephants killed hundreds of them, and in a few minutes the Roman army was put to flight.

It was saved from entire destruction by only one thing. A Roman soldier was brave enough to rush at an elephant while it was charging and cut off a part of its trunk with his sword. The animal, wild with pain, turned and ran back to the Greek lines, trampling down the soldiers and causing a great deal of confusion. In the excitement the Romans managed to escape across a river to a friendly city where they were safe.

Pyrrhus won the victory, but he lost thousands of men. When he saw the great number of his soldiers that lay dead on the field, he exclaimed:

"A few more such victories and I must return to Epirus alone!"

III

Shortly after the battle Pyrrhus sent his friend and favorite minister, Cin'e-as, to Rome to offer terms of peace to the Senate. Cineas was a very eloquent man. Often when Pyrrhus could not conquer people in battle, Cineas by his clever speeches induced them to submit to the king and be his friends. This was why the Greeks used to say, "The tongue of Cineas wins more cities than the sword of Pyrrhus."

Cineas proposed to the Roman Senate that the Romans should not make war any longer on the Tarentines, nor on any of the Italian tribes that had helped them, and that all the lands Rome had taken from these tribes in past years should be given back. If the Romans would agree to these terms, then Pyrrhus would be their true friend.

The terms were not good for Rome, but Cineas was so smooth-spoken and so pleasant in proposing them that many of the senators were inclined to accept them. One day while they were discussing the matter in the Senate a thrilling scene occurred.

Appius Claudius was still living in Rome. He was very old and had become blind. For this reason he got the name *Cœ'cus,* a word which is Latin for *blind.* But his mind was remarkably clear, and he had not lost interest in public affairs. When he heard that the Senate was going to accept the terms offered by Pyrrhus he rose from his bed declaring that he would go and speak against the proposal.

So he was carried by his slaves to the Senate house, and his sons led the aged man to his seat. He began his speech amidst the deepest silence. His youth seemed to come back to him. Once more he was the bold censor of thirty years before. In fiery words he spoke against the plan for peace, saying it would be base and cowardly to yield to the Greek king.

"Let us fight on," he said, "as long as we have soldiers. Shall we submit to this Greek invader merely because we have lost one battle? Never! Never! I say. Better to lose all that we have than to disgrace ourselves by submitting!"

The patriotic old man went on speaking in this way until his strength failed him and he sank exhausted into his seat. His speech had so much effect on the senators that they immediately voted against the proposal of Pyrrhus and ordered Cineas to depart from Rome.

Then the war was carried on vigorously. A great battle was fought at As'cu-lum, and again the Romans were defeated by the Greeks. But they were not discouraged. The Consul Cu'ri-us Den-ta'tus fought another battle against Pyrrhus at Ben'e-ven'tum, and won a glorious victory. The Greeks were utterly defeated, and Pyrrhus soon afterwards left Italy and returned to his own country.

Then the Romans speedily took possession of Tarentum and made its people pay well for their insult to the Roman ambassadors.

REGULUS

I

The next great war the Romans engaged in was with Carthage. It was about the possession of the island of Sicily, in the Mediterranean Sea. It began not long after Pyrrhus left Italy and was the first of three wars called the Pu'nic Wars. Punic means Phœ-ni'ci-an and the people who founded Carthage came from Phœ-ni'ci-a, so Carthage was called a Punic or Phœnician colony.

When the first Punic War began both Rome and Carthage were very rich and powerful. Rome had great armies and great generals. Its common soldiers, too, were remarkably brave and patriotic. It was very successful in its wars. Before it began to fight Carthage it had conquered nearly all Italy.

Carthage, also, had fine armies, but its greatest strength was in its navy. No other country in the world at that time had so many ships of war and trading ships. The ships of the Carthaginians went everywhere in the Mediterranean. Some of them even went past the Pillars of Hercules, as the rocky capes at the Strait of Gibraltar were then called, and sailed for some distance on the Atlantic Ocean.

The Carthaginian ships were small, but they were very strong. The warships were built to carry a good many soldiers, as well as sailors and oarsmen. They had great rounded iron prows, which could do much damage to an enemy's ships when run up against them. Each ship had a mast and large sail, but it was also rowed with oars by many oarsmen who sat on long benches, placed one above the other. With the sail and the oars the ship could be made to go very fast through the water.

Carthage was in North Africa, in the country now called Tunisia. It stood at the head of a beautiful bay of the Mediterranean. It was a large and handsome city and had a great commerce.

II

Many years before the beginning of the first Punic War Cathage conquered a great part of Sicily and made it a Carthaginian colony. But the Romans wanted the island, and so under the pretence of protecting an Italian tribe that had settled there they sent an army into Sicily. This was how the first Punic War began.

Both Rome and Carthage fought fiercely, and for a long time neither had much advantage over the other. At first the Romans had no warships. Up to that time they did not need any, for all their fighting was on land. But when they began war with the Carthaginians they found that they must have ships to carry their soldiers to Sicily and to fight the Carthaginians at sea. So the Romans set to work to build ships and to train men to row them, and in a short time they had a great navy.

In the ninth year of the war the armies and fleets of Rome were put under the command of a general named Marcus A-til'i-us Reg'u-lus. He was a great hero and patri-ot. He had been a general before the Punic War and had often led the Romans to victory. After years of good ser-vice, fighting and winning battles for his country, he went to live on his little farm and, like Cincinnatus, he cultivat-ed it with his own hands. A story is told of him which well illustrates ancient Roman honor and patriotism.

Until Regulus took command the Punic War was carried on only in Sicily and on the Mediterranean. But he thought that Rome should fight the Carthaginians in their own country, and so he organized an immense army and navy to invade Carthage. He had three hundred and thirty warships of the largest size and about sixty thousand soldiers.

In those times, in fights at sea, they had an engine called a boarding bridge. One end of it was fixed to the deck of the ship. The other end, which was free, could be swung round and on to an enemy's ship, and it had a heavy iron spike underneath, so that when it fell on the deck it would sink into it and thus hold the enemy's vessel for the attacking party to board it.

When everything was ready Regulus set sail for Africa. Soon after starting he met a large Carthaginian fleet, and in a short battle he destroyed it. Then he sailed on and after landing in Africa began a march towards Carthage. On his way he captured several towns, and he met and defeated a Carthaginian army. He then continued his march until he met another army of Carthaginians. This army was commanded by Xan-thip'pus, a famous general of Sparta, in Greece, who happened to be in Carthage at that time. In the battle that followed the Romans were defeated, and Regulus was made prisoner and taken off to Carthage.

III

But the Romans had other generals and other armies, and they carried on the war and defeated the Carthaginians in many battles.

At last the Carthaginians thought it better to try to make peace, and so they sent ambassadors to Rome to propose that the war should be stopped on certain terms, which they were ready to offer. They sent Regulus with the ambassadors, but they made him swear that he would return to Carthage if the Roman Senate should refuse to agree to their terms. They thought that in order to gain his own freedom Regulus would try to get the Senate to accept their proposals. Regulus agreed to go and made the promise required.

"I give you my word of honor," said he, "that I will return if your terms are not accepted."

Then he set out for Rome with the ambassadors. As he approached the gates of the city, thousands of people came forth to welcome him and to escort him through the streets. But he refused to enter.

"I cannot enter Rome," said he. "I am no longer a Roman officer, but a prisoner of Carthage. Do not urge me to enter the gates. I am not even worth exchanging for a Carthaginian prisoner."

The people, however, insisted that he should enter the city, and so amid shouts and cheers he was escorted to the Senate house.

In a little while the Carthaginian ambassadors presented their proposals, and the Senate began to consider them. After some discussion Regulus was asked to give his opinion whether the terms ought to be accepted or not.

Regulus at first was unwilling to speak in the Senate. He said that by becoming a prisoner he had lost the honor of being a senator.

"I am no longer a Roman senator," said he. "I am a prisoner of Carthage."

The Senate, however, insisted that he should speak. Then Regulus said that the Senate ought not to accept the terms of peace offered by Carthage. He thought that they were not good terms for Rome, and he advised the Senate not to agree to them.

But the Senate was inclined to accept the terms for the sake of Regulus himself. If peace were not made he would have to go back and remain a prisoner in Carthage, or perhaps he would be put to death. Therefore the Senate was for agreeing to the Carthaginian terms. But Regulus again spoke strongly against them, and at last the Senate decided to reject the Carthaginian proposals.

IV

Regulus now prepared to return to Carthage, but his family and friends clung to him, saying:

"You must not go! You must not go!"

To all their appeals he made but one answer:

"I have given my word of honor to return, and I cannot break it."

So Regulus returned to Carthage with the ambassadors. When the people of that city heard that by his advice their terms had been rejected they were very angry. They had wished very much to make peace with Rome, for the long war had cost them a great many lives and a great deal of money, and they wanted to stop it. Therefore they were enraged against Regulus and they put him to death in a very cruel way.

The war between Rome and Carthage continued for some years more, but at last the Carthaginians were defeated in a great sea battle near the coast of Sicily. They were then obliged to give up Sicily and pay a large sum of money to the Romans as a fine. This was the end of the first Punic War (241 B.C.).

SCIPIO AFRICANUS

I

But peace did not last long between Rome and Carthage. Some years after the end of the first Punic War the Carthaginians attacked and took possession of a town in Spain, the people of which were friends and allies of Rome. This caused the second Punic War, which began 218 B.C.

One of the great soldiers of this war was Pub'li-us Cornelius Scip'i-o. In the latter part of his life he was called Scipio Af-ri-ca'nus, on account of the great victories which he won in Africa.

Scipio was a brave soldier from his youth. When only seventeen years old he fought in a battle and saved his father's life. He was always gallant and heroic in war, so he soon became noted in the Roman army and rose to high rank. And although he was a member of a noble family, he was well liked by the plebeians and they elected him "ædile."

The ædiles were magistrates or judges. They were also superintendents of public buildings and of the games and shows of which the Roman people were so fond.

When Scipio was about twenty-seven years of age, he was appointed to command the Roman army that was fighting the Carthaginians in Spain. Carthage had conquered some parts of Spain, and Rome had conquered other parts, and the two nations were often at war about places in that country.

When Scipio went to Spain many of the people there were against him, but they soon became his friends. Whenever he took a city he allowed the chiefs who were captured to go free, and he gave presents to many of them. He always showed great respect to women and children who were taken prisoners. In those times it was the cruel custom to make slaves of women who were found in towns that had been taken in war. But Scipio never did this in Spain. He always let the women go free.

One day a beautiful Spanish girl who had been taken prisoner was brought before him. She seemed very much frightened, but Scipio spoke kindly to her and told her that no one should harm her. While speaking with her he learned that a young man who was her lover had also been taken prisoner by the Roman soldiers. He sent for the young man and said to him:

"Take your sweetheart and go. I set you both free. Go and be happy and in future be friends of Rome."

And so by many acts of kindness Scipio gained the friendship of the Spaniards. After a while they began to join the Romans and gave them great help in their war against the Carthaginians.

II

When his services were no longer needed in Spain, Scipio returned to Rome. He got a great reception in the city. There was a grand parade in his honor. He brought home an immense quantity of silver, which he obtained from the rich Spanish mines and from the cities he had taken. The silver was put into the Roman treasury to pay the expenses of the war.

Soon after he returned from Spain Scipio was elected consul. The Carthaginian general, Han'ni-bal, was then in Italy with a large army. This Hannibal was one of the greatest generals of ancient times. When he was but nine years old his father, who was also a great general, made him take an oath that he would hate Rome and the Romans forever. Then he took the boy with him to Spain and gave him a thorough training as a soldier.

When his father died Hannibal became commander of the Carthaginian army in Spain. He was then little more than twenty-one years old. He fought well in Spain for some time and was well liked by his soldiers. Suddenly he resolved to make war on the Romans in their own country and to go by land to Italy. So he got ready an immense army and set out on his march. In passing through France he had to cross the broad River Rhone. This was not easy to do, for there was no bridge. He got his men over in boats, but he had a number of elephants in his army and they were too big and heavy to be taken across in that way. The boats were small and the elephants were afraid to go into them. Hannibal therefore got rafts or floats, made of trunks of trees tied together, and in these the elephants were carried over.

After crossing the Rhone Hannibal marched over the Alps into Italy. He and his army suffered many hardships in making their way over those snow-covered mountains. He had often to fight fierce tribes that came to oppose him, but he defeated them all, and after being defeated many of them joined his army and brought him provisions for his soldiers.

Very soon Roman armies were sent against Hannibal, but he defeated them in many battles. Once his army got into a place near high hills where he could not march further except through one narrow pass between the hills. The Roman general, Quintus Fabius, sent four thousand of his troops to take possession of this pass, and he posted the rest of his army on the hills close by.

Hannibal saw that he was in a trap, but he found a way of escaping. He caused vine branches to be tied to the horns of a large number of the oxen that were with his army. Then he ordered his men to set the branches on fire in the middle of the night and to drive the oxen up the hills.

As soon as the animals felt the pain they rushed madly

about and set fire to the shrubs and bushes they met on the way. The Romans at the pass thought that the Carthaginians were escaping by torchlight. So they hastily quit their posts and hurried towards the hills to help their comrades. Then Hannibal, seeing the pass free, marched his army out and so escaped from the trap.

Quintus Fabius was very slow and cautious in his movements. The Romans had been defeated so often that he thought the best plan was to harass Hannibal in every possible way, but not to venture to fight him in a great battle until he should be sure of winning. For this reason the Romans gave Fabius the name of *Cunc-ta'tor*, which means *delayer*, and so the plan of extreme delay or caution in any undertaking is often called a *Fabian* policy.

But in spite of the caution of Fabius Hannibal gained many great victories. His greatest victory was at the battle of Can'næ, in the south of Italy. Here he defeated and destroyed a Roman army of seventy thousand men. And for several years after this battle Hannibal remained in Italy doing the Romans all the harm he could.

At last Scipio thought it was time to follow the plan of Regulus. So he said to the Senate:

"We have acted too long as if we were afraid of Hannibal and Carthage. We defend ourselves bravely when we are attacked, and so far we have saved Rome from destruction; but we do not make any attacks on our enemies. We certainly ought to do this, for our armies are strong and fully ready to meet the Carthaginians."

Scipio then proposed that an army led by himself should go to Africa and carry on war there. He believed that if this were done Hannibal would have to go to Africa to defend Carthage.

Perhaps on account of what had happened to Regulus, the Senate did not like Scipio's plan. Nevertheless, it gave him permission to go to Africa, but would not give him an army. Scipio then raised a splendid army of volunteers and sailed across the Mediterranean Sea to Africa.

III

Scipio tried for some time to obtain the aid of Sy'phax, a powerful king of Nu-mid'i-a, in Africa. But Syphax decided to join the Carthaginians. So Scipio found two great armies ready to fight him. One was the army of Carthage, with thirty-three thousand men, commanded by Has'dru-bal Gis'co, and the other was the army of Numidia, with sixty thousand men, commanded by King Syphax.

But Scipio found in Africa one strong friend, and that was a Numidian prince named Mas'i-nis'sa. This prince had a host of supporters among his countrymen and was therefore able to bring a large force of good soldiers to the aid of the Romans. He was of great service to Scipio in many ways.

When everything was ready the Roman army, with Masinissa's force, encamped about six miles from the camps of the enemy. Scipio sent spies among the Carthaginians and the soldiers of King Syphax, and from them he learned that both armies were lodged in huts made of stakes and covered with reeds and dried leaves. He resolved to set those huts on fire.

So one very dark night the Roman army left its camp and marched silently to the plain occupied by the enemy. Then a division of the Romans went to the encampment of the Numidians and a soldier crept cautiously from the Roman lines and set one of the huts on fire. The fire spread rapidly, and in a few minutes the whole camp was in flames.

The Numidian soldiers, suddenly awakened by the fire, fled from the burning huts without their weapons and made frantic efforts to escape from the camp. Hundreds of them were knocked down and trampled to death in the rush and confusion; hundreds more lost their lives in the fire. Those who got to the open country were attacked by the Romans and killed. The ground was covered with the bodies of the slain. King Syphax and a few horsemen managed to escape, but the rest of the vast Numidian army was destroyed.

In the meantime the Carthaginians had been aroused by the noise in the camp of the Numidians. They thought that the fire had been caused by an accident, and some of them ran forward to assist the Numidians. But the greater number stood in a confused throng, without their arms, outside their camp, looking at the fire with terror.

While they were in this helpless state the Carthaginians were suddenly attacked by the Romans with Scipio at their head. Many were killed, and the others were driven back into their camp, which was immediately set on fire in a number of places. Then there was a frightful scene. Thousands of Carthaginians, struggling to escape the fire, were slain by the Romans, while thousands more perished in the flames. Hasdrubal Gisco, the commander, and some of his officers escaped, but only a few of the others. In less than an hour there was little left of the Carthaginian army.

IV

Scipio now began to march towards the great, rich city of Carthage. He captured a number of towns and a great deal of treasure. In a few weeks, however, the Carthaginians were able to form another army of thirty thousand men, and then they came boldly forth to meet Scipio.

A fierce battle followed. The Romans were driven back for a time, but with wonderful courage they charged the Carthaginians again and again and at last totally defeated them.

The Carthaginians now sent a message to Italy requesting Hannibal to come to the relief of his country. The renowned general did not want to leave Italy, for he hoped to be able to take Rome; but he thought it best to obey the call of Carthage, so he sailed for Africa with his army.

After arriving in Africa Hannibal led his army to a wide plain near Za'ma, a town not far from Carthage. Here he awaited the Romans.

Hannibal had great admiration for Scipio, and he

desired to see him before engaging in battle. So he sent a messenger to Scipio requesting an interview. The request was granted, and the two generals met.

They greeted each other cordially, and each complimented the other on his victories and greatness as a soldier. Then Hannibal proposed terms of peace to Scipio.

"We will give Spain and the islands of Sicily and Sardinia to Rome. Then we will divide the sea with you. What more would you have? Rome and Carthage would then be the two great nations of the world."

Scipio thought it was too late to make terms.

"We must fight it out," said he, "until one side or the other is vanquished."

The generals then parted, and the next day the two armies were drawn up in battle array. On each side there were about thirty thousand men, but Hannibal had a herd of fighting elephants.

The battle was long and severe. Both armies fought heroically, and there was terrible slaughter. But Hannibal's elephants were of little use to him, as the Romans frightened them by blowing trumpets and hurling balls of fire at them. At a moment when the lines of the Carthaginians were breaking, a strong force of Roman horsemen came up suddenly in the rear and overpowered all before it. This won the battle for the Romans. When Hannibal saw that the battle was lost he fled from the field with a few friends (202 B.C.).

Scipio was now master of Carthage. He compelled the Carthaginians to pay him a vast amount in gold and silver and to give up some of their towns and lands. He also compelled them to destroy their great fleet of warships and to promise not to make war in future upon any people without the permission of the Romans.

When Scipio returned to Rome he entered the city at the head of a grand procession. The greatest honors were paid to him, and he was called Scipio Africanus.

Some years afterwards Scipio met Hannibal at the court of the king of Syria. The two generals had a friendly conversation and Scipio asked Hannibal who he thought was the greatest general that ever lived. Hannibal answered:

"Alexander the Great."

"Who was the second?" asked Scipio.

"Pyrrhus," replied Hannibal.

"Who the third?"

"Myself," answered Hannibal.

"But what would you have said," asked Scipio, "if you had conquered me?"

"I should then have said," replied Hannibal, "that I was greater than Alexander, greater than Pyrrhus, and greater than all other generals."

CATO THE CENSOR

I

On a farm near Tusculum, a little town about fifteen miles from Rome, there once lived a boy named Mar'cus Por'ci-us Ca'to. His father and his grandfather before him had been farmers and he, too, expected to be one.

When he was about seventeen Hannibal's army crossed the Alps into Italy, and young Cato became a Roman soldier. When the war ended the country boy had become a man, stern and forceful. He attracted the attention of a neighbor, a rich man, who persuaded him to go to Rome and practice law.

In time he was elected to office, and he did his duty so well that he rose higher and higher, until he became one of the consuls. That same year a rebellion arose in Spain, and Cato led an army against the Spaniards. It is said that in four hundred days he captured four hundred villages. On his return to Rome he was honored with a triumph.

Shortly after this he was sent to Greece, where An-ti'o-chus was attacking Greek cities that were friendly to Rome. He defeated Antiochus in the Pass of Thermopylae and won great fame as a soldier.

Cato was a very hard man; hard on himself, hard on his friends. And although he was rich and held office in a great city, he lived a hard life, taking no pleasures and saving his money. He ate the plainest food and drank the same cheap wine that he bought for his slaves.

He thought that the luxury and extravagance of the rich were taking away the strength of Rome. In order to put a stop to these things Cato asked the people of Rome to elect him censor. The patricians opposed him bitterly, but he was elected by a large majority. One of the first things he did was to expel from the Senate several senators who were leading improper lives. He had a heavy tax put on carriages so as to compel people to walk. He also placed a tax on jewels, handsome dresses, carpets, and fine furniture. So well did he do his work that he is always known in history as Cato the Censor, just as if he were the only man who ever held the office. A statue erected in his honor says nothing about his victories in Spain or at Thermopylae, but only that, "When the Roman Republic was degenerating, Cato restored it by strict discipline."

II

In the later years of his life Cato was sent to Carthage to look into a certain matter for Rome. The trouble was this: You will remember that Carthage had agreed to make war upon no nation without the consent of the Roman Senate. A few years later, Masinissa, who was a friend of Rome, attacked the Carthaginians, and they appealed to Rome for protection. This was refused, and the people of Carthage took up arms to defend themselves against Masinissa.

Cato was sent to Carthage to find out who was to blame. When he arrived in the city he was surprised to find it large and strong and flourishing. Only twenty-six years had passed since Scipio Africanus had conquered Carthage, and yet Cato saw crowds of young men on the street, stacks of arms in the arsenals, and a forest of masts in the harbor. The city itself was rich and prosperous.

Cato returned to Rome and warned his countrymen that Carthage must be destroyed. From that time forward whenever he made a speech in the Senate, no matter upon what subject, he always ended it by saying, "And my opinion is that Carthage must be destroyed." In time, the words of Cato had their effect, and war was declared against Carthage.

The troops had already embarked when envoys from Carthage reached Rome and offered to do whatever might be asked. The Roman Senate promised that the laws and liberties of Carthage should not be touched, but demanded hostages. So three hundred children of the leading families of Carthage were sent to Rome. When the Roman army reached Carthage the consuls insisted that the Carthaginians should give up their arms. This was done and the Carthaginians asked if the Romans required anything more.

Then one of the consuls said, "Your city must be destroyed, and you must move ten miles inland from the sea." The Carthaginians now saw that they had been deceived. They closed their gates and determined to defend themselves to the last. They asked an armistice of thirty days, so that an embassy might go to Rome. It was granted, and thus a month of time was gained. During this time men, women, and children went to work to make arms to defend their homes. The women even cut off their hair to furnish strings for the bows of the war machines with which stones were hurled at the enemy.

The embassy failed in its mission to Rome and the siege of Carthage began. It lasted three years.

The son of Paulus Æ-mil'i-us had been adopted by the son of Scipio Africanus and had taken the name Scipio. He was sent to Carthage and about a year after his arrival forced an entrance into the city and captured it (146 B.C.). The walls were torn down and the buildings set on fire. Cato who was so largely responsible for the war did not live to see its end. He died almost two years before the city was destroyed.

The Senate honored Scipio with the title Africanus, which the older conqueror of Carthage had borne.

The young Scipio won fame not only in Africa but also in Spain, where he was sent against the Numantians.

These brave people had defeated two Roman armies, but Scipio soon succeeded in shutting them within the walls of Numantia. Around its walls he built walls of his own behind which his soldiers were safe from attack. Food soon became scarce in Numantia. At the end of fifteen months the citizens were starving. They were willing to lose their lives, but Scipio stayed behind his own walls and refused to fight. Rather than trust to the mercy of Rome the Numantians killed themselves.

In time all Spain was forced to submit and become a Roman province.

THE GRACCHI

I

Between the second and third Punic Wars there lived in Rome two brothers named Ti-be'ri-us and Caius Grac'chus, commonly called the Gracchi. They were very good men and great friends of the common people.

The mother of the Gracchi was Cor-ne'li-a, a daughter of Scipio Africanus. She was an excellent woman, and she was very proud of her two sons. She taught them to be brave and manly and always to stand up for the people.

One day a rich lady, while on a visit to Cornelia, showed her some magnificent jewels. When they had looked them over the lady said:

"These are my jewels; now let me see yours."

Just at that moment Tiberius and Caius, who were then boys, came into the room. As soon as she saw them Cornelia called them to her and, putting her arms around them, said:

"These are my jewels."

When Tiberius and Caius grew up to be men they took the side of the people in a quarrel that had been going on for a long time between the plebeians and the nobles. The quarrel was about land. Whenever the Romans conquered a country in war they took possession of a portion of the land of the conquered country. Such land was called public land, and for many years after the founding of the city the custom of dividing parts of the public lands among all the citizens was strictly observed.

But in later times this custom was changed. Instead of part of the public lands being divided among all the citizens, it was divided among only the nobles, and the plebeians got none at all. The lands were tilled by slaves, and all that was raised went to the nobles. So the poor soldiers who won the lands by hard fighting were without farms to till, and some of them even without homes. They continually demanded that the old law, for a fair division of the lands among all the citizens, should be carried out. The nobles laughed at the demand.

But Tiberius Gracchus came forward boldly as the champion of the poor. He declared that the nobles should give up the lands they had unjustly taken, and that the people should have their fair share. His words made the nobles very angry, and they became his bitter enemies.

II

But the people honored Tiberius and made him one of their tribunes. The tribunes were supposed to look after the people's interests, but sometimes they were not faithful to their duty. As we have already said, they had a great deal of power. They could sit at the door of the Roman Senate, and when a law was proposed that they did not like they could say, "We veto it!" and then the law could not be passed.

Whenever the tribunes wanted a law passed they proposed it at the meeting of all the people in what was called the Assembly of Tribes. The common people had a great deal of power in this Assembly, and any law proposed by the tribune was generally passed. Then the tribunes had the power to compel the consuls to carry out the law.

Not long after Tiberius Gracchus became tribune he proposed a law that each noble might have five hundred acres of the public land for his own use and two hundred and fifty more for each son, and that the remainder of the lands should be equally divided among the poor citizens.

This law was passed, and then the nobles had to give up

a large part of the lands they had seized. So the poor citizens got good farms.

About this time At'ta-lus, the king of Per'ga-mus, a country of Asia, died, leaving all his money to the Romans. The nobles tried to get this money for themselves, but Tiberius had it divided among the poor citizens.

Of course this made the nobles still more angry with Tiberius, and they resolved to get rid of him if they could. So on election day, when the people were voting to make Tiberius tribune for a second term, some nobles went to the voting-place and raised a disturbance. But the friends of Tiberius drove them away. Then the nobles started a report that Tiberius was trying to induce the people to make him king.

Afterwards they gathered their friends and slaves and began fighting with the people. No arms were used, but stones were thrown, and sticks, broken benches, and other things hastily caught up, served as weapons. There was a dreadful tumult for a while, and many persons were killed.

Tiberius was in the midst of his friends bravely defending himself against an attack by a party of nobles, when suddenly he stumbled and fell to the ground. In a moment the nobles rushed upon him. One of them struck him on the head with a piece of wood and killed him. Then they took his body and threw it into the Tiber.

III

Tiberius was now out of the way, and the nobles began to seize the lands that had been divided among the people. But Caius Gracchus suddenly appeared in Rome and declared that he had come to take his brother's place as the friend of the people. He had been with a Roman army in Spain when Tiberius was killed.

The people now elected him tribune and he began to carry out his brother's plans. For this reason the nobles hated him as much as they had hated his brother. They said that he was a dangerous man and was planning to make himself king. One day as he was passing through the Forum a strange man said to him:

"I hope you will spare the Republic!"

The friends of Caius were angry at these words, and they fell on the man and killed him.

The nobles and their followers then armed themselves. The plebeians also gathered in great numbers ready for a fight. Caius was asked to lead them, but refused. He did not want them to fight with the nobles. He knew that the nobles would be satisfied with his own death, so he ordered a slave to stab him to the heart. The order was obeyed, and thus perished the last of the Gracchi (121 B.C.).

MARIUS

I

At the time of the death of Caius Gracchus there was in Rome a great man named Caius Ma'ri-us. This man came forward and said to the people that if they would elect him tribune he would get them their rights.

The people elected him tribune and, true to his word, he did everything he could to improve their condition. He was afterwards elected consul seven times, and for a long while he was the greatest man in Rome.

Marius was a tall and very powerful man and had a strong will. When he said he would do anything he would do it in spite of all difficulties. He was a very great soldier. Many people thought him the best of the Roman generals.

He succeeded in a war against Ju-gur'tha, king of Numidia, after other generals had failed. He took many cities from Jugurtha and at last captured the king himself and all his treasure.

Jugurtha was brought to Rome and compelled to walk behind the chariot of Marius in a grand triumphal procession. He was afterwards put into a foul dungeon and left there to die.

The nobles did not like Marius. He was the son of plebeian parents and he had taken the side of the plebeians against the nobles. Therefore the nobles hated him, and they would have done everything they could against him, only that they needed his help to protect Rome from very dangerous enemies.

A host of barbarian people, called Cim'bri, Teu'to-nes, and Am-bro'nes, had left their homes on the shores of the Baltic Sea and invaded the southern lands. They were strong, fierce men, and they laid waste every country they passed through. They defeated several Roman armies that were sent against them. Some of the tribes of Hel-ve'ti-a (the country now called Switzerland) joined them and one of those tribes defeated and killed a Roman consul and made his army pass under the yoke.

The Romans were, therefore, very much frightened. They thought that the barbarians would soon be in Italy. So Marius was appointed to go against them with a great army. He crossed the Mediterranean into Gaul and met the Teutones and Ambrones near the city of Arles on the River Rhone. The Cimbri had already gone to Italy.

Marius first made a strong entrenched camp. He wanted to give his men time to get accustomed to the manners of the strange enemy before attempting to fight them. The Roman soldiers had shown fear at sight of the barbarians. They had never before seen such people.

The Teutones were like giants. They had large, wild, staring eyes and long hair, and they made terrible warcries. The Ambrones and the Cimbri were as savage in appearance. The king of the Teutones was very tall and so active that he could leap over six horses placed abreast.

When the barbarians saw that the Romans would not fight, they began to taunt and insult them. They walked up and down in front of the Roman camp day after day, calling the soldiers cowards.

"Why don't you come out and fight us like men?" they cried. "Are you afraid? Come out, come out; we are in a hurry! We are going to Rome after we kill you!"

Marius had hard work to keep his men from rushing out upon the barbarians. He did not yet want to fight, but he said to his soldiers:

"When the proper time comes we will give these savages all the fighting they want."

One day a gigantic Teuton chief, with a long shield and

spear, came up to the very entrance of the Roman camp and called loudly for Marius himself to come out and fight. The great general laughed heartily at the impudence of the barbarian, and he sent out a gladiator to fight with him in order to give sport to the Romans.

Gladiators were men who fought one another in the shows at Rome for the amusement of the people. They were usually slaves and were very strong, active, and well-trained fighters.

It did not take the gladiator long to defeat the Teuton. In a few minutes he laid the savage giant low, and the Romans shouted with joy at the sight.

After the Teuton was killed the Romans still remained in their camp. Marius was not yet prepared to fight. At last the barbarians got tired of waiting and they started off to march to Italy.

II

So great was the number of the barbarians that it took them six whole days to march past the Roman camp. When all had passed Marius left his camp and followed them by slow marches. Before long the two armies arrived at the city of Aix on the south coast of Gaul.

Marius thought it was now time to fight, so he led out his fine army against the enemy. The first battle was fought with the Ambrones. They astonished the Romans with their war-cry. They held their shields upright and at a little distance from their mouths and shouted: "Ambrones! Ambrones!" as if to terrify the Romans by letting them know who they were. Then they rushed furiously across the field.

The Romans met the charge with wonderful courage. Their lines were scarcely broken. Three times they drove back the enemy, and then they themselves moved steadily forward with their whole force. They cut down the Ambrones by thousands, took many prisoners, and sent the others fleeing away in terror.

Next day there was another battle. The Teutones and Ambrones together attacked the Romans, but the Romans were again victorious. When the battle was over it was found that more than a hundred thousand barbarians had been killed or taken prisoner.

Marius now turned his attention to the Cimbri, who had gone to Italy. They had encamped on a beautiful, fertile plain near the River Po, and were enjoying the warm Italian sun and the sweet fruits of the country.

But Marius was not very long in reaching the same place with his victorious army. When the Cimbri saw the Romans marching on to the plain where they were encamped, they were astonished. To gain time they sent a messenger to Marius to ask him to give them lands to live on in Italy.

"Give us," said the messenger, "lands in Italy for ourselves and for our friends, the Teutones and Ambrones, and we will all live at peace."

"Never mind the Teutones and the Ambrones," said Marius, "they have lands already. We have given them some which they will keep forever. We will give you the same."

Then a battle began between the two great armies. The foot soldiers of the Cimbri were formed into an immense square, and the men in the front ranks were chained to one another by iron chains so that they could not run away. There were fifteen thousand horsemen, wearing on their helmets the heads of wild beasts.

The battle was a hard one for a while, but it did not continue long. Time after time the Cimbri were driven back, and at last they were put to flight. Thousands of them were killed, and thousands made prisoners.

When Marius and his soldiers returned to Rome they got a splendid reception. There was a parade through the streets, and a great feast was given to the people. A large sum of money was divided among the soldiers to reward them for their brave conduct.

Marius was now in high favor at Rome. The nobles did

not dare to speak a word against him. He was elected consul seven times, so that he was master of the Republic for
a long time.

In the sixth year that Marius was consul the war called
the Social War broke out. It lasted for three years. It was a
war with some of the nations of Italy which Rome had formerly conquered. The people of those nations did not
want to separate from Rome, but they wanted to have the
right of voting as the Romans themselves had. Rome
refused to give them this right, and at last they resolved
to go to war.

All the greatest Roman generals of the time took part in
this war. One of them was a young noble named Sul'la. He
was a very successful soldier and won a number of great
victories. The nations were defeated in the war, but Rome
soon granted them most of the rights they had asked for.

The nobles gave great praise to Sulla for his victories in
the Social War. They declared that he was a better general than Marius. So many fine things were said about the
young noble that Marius became jealous and did a very
foolish thing. He suddenly left his army in the field and
came back to Rome. He complained that he was nervous
and he shut himself up in his house and refused to see any
of his friends for weeks.

The nobles then started a story that Marius was getting
silly and weak-minded from old age. He was about seventy at this time, and the nobles said he ought to retire from
the army. This made the old hero angry and he declared
he was as strong in mind and body as any of the young
Romans.

One morning he went to the place where the young men
of Rome used to practise athletic sports, and for two or
three hours he wrestled and ran and leaped with as much
skill and strength as any one. Some of the nobles who happened to pass by saw him and were very much amused.

About this time Sulla was elected consul on account of
his victories in the Social War. Shortly afterwards Rome
declared war against Mith'ri-da'tes, King of Pontus in Asia

Minor, who had cruelly put to death a number of the citizens of a Roman province in Asia.

The Senate appointed Sulla to command the Roman army in this war. But as soon as he left Rome with his army one of the tribunes proposed at an Assembly of the people that the command should be taken from him and given to Marius. The Assembly agreed to this and Marius accepted the appointment. He sent word to the army, which was not far from Rome, that he would come in a short time to take command.

When Sulla heard this he became very angry. He called his soldiers around him, told them what had been done, and asked them if they would submit to be the slaves of Marius and his party.

"No, no!" cried the soldiers, "we will not submit. We want you for our general."

"Then follow me to Rome," said Sulla, "we will teach Marius and his friends that they must not insult us."

So the soldiers marched quickly back to Rome with Sulla at their head. They declared that they would take the city out of the hands of rebels, as they called the friends of Marius. When they entered the city they were met by Marius and his followers and there was a battle, in which Marius was defeated. Then a law was passed declaring Marius a traitor and that he should be put to death.

But Marius fled from Rome with some friends and went down the Tiber in a boat to the Mediterranean. He sailed along the coast and then he and his companions went ashore to seek for food. They wandered through the country for some time without seeing any one. At last they met a farmer, who gave them something to eat. He told them that horsemen from Rome were riding through the place searching for Marius.

They were frightened at this and they ran into a thick wood where they stopped all night. But while his companions were downcast Marius was cheerful and hopeful.

"This bad state of things," he said, "will last only a short time. I know it, because the gods have revealed to me that I shall be once more consul of Rome!"

But next day Marius was taken by the horsemen. He saw them coming and waded far into a great marsh and hid himself among some high, thick reeds. The horsemen rode into the marsh and found him, and they put a rope round his neck and dragged him to the shore. Then they shut him up in a hut and began to think what they should do with him.

At last they decided to put him to death at once. They thought this would please Sulla, and that perhaps he would reward them for it. So they gave a sword to a slave and sent him to kill Marius. The slave entered the hut and stood for a few moments looking at the great general. Marius glared at him like a wild beast and said in a stern voice:

"Slave, will you dare to kill Caius Marius?"

The slave started back in terror and ran out of the hut. Then he threw down his sword at the feet of the soldiers and cried out that he could never have the courage to slay Marius.

It was now decided to send Marius out of the country. So he was taken to a ship and carried to Africa. After going ashore he wandered through the country until he came to the place where Carthage once stood. Nothing now remained of the famous city but a mass of gloomy ruins, for the Romans had entirely destroyed it a few years before in the third Punic War. In these ruins Marius lived for a short time. One day a soldier came to tell him that the governor of Africa wanted him to leave the country.

"Go to your governor," answered Marius, "and tell him that you saw Caius Marius sitting on the ruins of Carthage."

Not long afterwards, when Sulla was away fighting King Mithridates, there was great trouble at Rome. One of the consuls named Cin'na, aided by many of the plebeians, attempted to get the control of public affairs, but was defeated by the nobles. Then Cinna and his followers were forced to leave the city. They organized an army among the Italians who had been complaining of not getting their rights from Rome, and they sent to Africa for Marius to come and be their commander.

When Marius arrived he made an attack on Rome and soon captured it. Then he marched in through the gates at the head of his army and took possession of the city. At the next election the people elected him consul.

Marius now resolved to have vengeance on the nobles who had driven him from Rome. And for several days the old Roman, surrounded by a guard of freed slaves, went through the city seeking the nobles in their houses, in the temples, in the Forum, and everywhere that they could be found, and killing them without mercy.

These were dreadful days. Some of the noblest men of Rome were put to death. None of Sulla's friends was spared. Even his wife and children were harshly treated and forced to leave the city.

Marius did not stop the bloody work until he had killed all his enemies that he could find. But his triumph was short. He died in a little more than two weeks after he had become consul for the seventh time.

SULLA

I

We have said something of Sulla, but there is much more to be told about him, for he was a very remarkable man, and he did remarkable things in Rome. His full name was Lu'ci-us Cornelius Sulla. He belonged to a very noble family. When he was a young man he was very fond of study and became an excellent scholar. He was also a good speaker and often made eloquent speeches in the Forum on public affairs.

He was a large, strong man, with red hair and a ruddy face. He was a very great soldier and one of the greatest of Roman generals. They called him "the Lion," he was so brave in battle, and he was so successful in war that he also got the name of *Felix*, a Latin word which means *happy* or fortunate.

II

One of the greatest wars that Sulla was in was a war against the Greeks. Rome had conquered Greece some time before, and the governors of many of the Greek cities were Romans. These governors were very cruel to the Greeks; therefore the people hated them. Mithridates, King of Pontus, knew this, and he offered to send armies to Greece to help to drive the Romans out of the country. The Greeks were very glad of this, and they prepared for war against the Romans.

Sulla arrived in Greece with a strong army and began a march through the country. He captured several of the cities and compelled them to submit to the Roman governors. Then he marched on to Athens, the capital city of Greece. But he found that it was occupied by Ar-che-la'us, one of the generals of King Mithridates, who had brought from Asia Minor an army to help the Greeks.

Athens at this time was one of the most strongly fortified cities in the world. Its walls were seventy feet high, and they were made of huge, thick blocks of hard, smooth stone. It took thousands of men many years to build these massive walls. The city was also well supplied with food, so that it could hold out against a siege for a long time.

For several weeks Sulla attacked Athens furiously day by day, but it was all in vain. He could not take the city. His soldiers tried many times to mount the high walls, but they could not do it.

At last Sulla had battering-rams made. These were engines for breaking down the walls of towns. They were long, heavy beams of wood, with iron at one end, formed like the head of a ram. This was why they were called battering-*rams*. At first they were worked by men with their hands and bodily strength. In later times they were hung from a cross beam, so as to swing back and forward, and the iron end was made to strike against the wall with great force.

When a number of battering-rams were ready, Sulla began another attack on Athens. But at dead of night a party of Athenians came out of the city and burned all the battering-rams. Sulla quickly had new ones made, and after months of hard labor the Romans at last succeeded in breaking down the walls and taking Athens. They plundered the beautiful city and destroyed many fine works of art. It is said that they carried off more than six hundred pounds of gold and silver.

Sulla remained in Athens only long enough to establish Roman authority there once more. Then he departed with his army and marched to Chær'o-ne'a, another town of

Greece, where there was a force of one hundred and twenty thousand men, which King Mithridates had sent to help the Greeks.

The Romans numbered only about forty thousand men, but Sulla was not afraid to fight the immense army of Mithridates. By placing his troops in good positions at the beginning of the battle, and afterwards by moving them skillfully from one point to another, he was able to win a great victory.

This was a remarkable battle in one respect. Although there were furious charges and hand-to-hand combats, in which thousands upon thousands of the soldiers of Mithridates were slain, the Romans lost only a few men. We are told that when the roll-call of the Roman army took place after the battle only twelve men failed to answer to their names! The army of Mithridates had lost one hundred and ten thousand men; the Romans only twelve men!

But perhaps we ought not to believe that so very few Romans were killed, for it seems hardly possible that it could have been so. It is certain, however, that Sulla gained a great victory. He also defeated another army sent by Mithridates soon afterwards.

Then Archelaus, the general of the army of Mithridates, begged for peace. Sulla made terms that were very good for Rome, and Archelaus and Mithridates had to accept them. Mithridates had to give the Romans a large sum of money and seventy ships of war and to promise to be the friend of Rome in future. Thus the war with Greece ended.

III

Sulla now prepared to return to Italy. He had heard how his friends in Rome and his wife and children had been treated by Marius. He was greatly enraged, and in his letter to the Senate, telling them of his victories in Greece, he said:

"In return for my services, which have brought honor and glory to Rome, my wife and children have been driven

from their home, my house has been burned, and my
friends have been put to death. I am now going back to
punish those who did these things."

When the letter was read to the senators, they were
very much alarmed, for they knew that if Sulla did as he
threatened it would cause a dreadful civil war in Rome. In
reply to Sulla they begged him not to make war on his own
countrymen, and they promised to do their best to bring
about a friendly understanding between him and the followers of Marius. Sulla answered that he did not want any
understanding with them.

"I want no friendship with my enemies," he said. "I am
able to take care of myself. It will be well for them if they
can take care of themselves."

Soon afterwards he set out for Italy with his army. Rome
was then under the power of the Marian party. This party
was led by Cinna and by Marius the Younger, the son of
the great Marius. When they heard that Sulla was coming
they raised an army and went forth to drive him back.
Young Marius said:

"Now it will be decided who shall be the master of
Rome!"

A battle was fought between the two armies. It was long
and severe, and for a time it seemed as if the Marians
would win. Even Sulla himself had no hope of victory. But
soon very bad blunders made by the Marians turned the
tide of battle in his favor, and he was victorious. He took
six thousand prisoners.

IV

Sulla now entered Rome as its master, and a cruel master
he proved to be. He first got himself appointed dictator
for as long a time as he wished to hold the office. Then he
commanded that all the followers of Marius should be
slain. So they were hunted out of their hiding places and
all put to death without mercy.

When every person that was known to have been connected with the Marian party was killed, the people thought Sulla would cease his murderous work, but he did not. He went on killing this one and that one—now a poor man and then a rich man—until at last the Romans became dreadfully frightened. "When will he stop?" they said to one another in trembling tones.

One day a senator had the courage to ask Sulla if he would please to say whom he intended to spare from death. Sulla coolly answered:

"I have not yet made up my mind, but if it is the wish of the Senate I will shortly make out a list of persons who must die!"

And Sulla really did make out a list of persons he intended to kill. It was called a PROSCRIPTION LIST and was hung up in the Forum. Oh, how anxiously the poor, terror-stricken Romans went to that list to read the names! And if a man saw that his name was not there he went away with joy in his heart. But if his name was there he covered his face with his toga and ran off to hide himself.

The next day another and a longer list of proscribed persons was hung up, and the day after still another list. Any one who killed a proscribed person got a large reward in money, but if anybody helped a proscribed person to escape he was punished by death. This dreadful work was continued until many thousands of people in Rome and throughout Italy were slain.

Then Sulla had his Triumph in the streets of Rome. It was the most magnificent procession that had yet been seen in the city. There were hundreds of beautiful horses drawing bright, golden chariots; there were long lines of soldiers in glittering armor; there were numbers of slaves, and there were huge wagons containing gold and silver and other precious things, which Sulla had got in Greece after his victories over Mithridates. The dictator himself rode in the most splendid chariot of all. He seemed like a king, and indeed was a king in power, though not in name. This was what was called a Triumph.

Sulla, for his own protection, had a bodyguard formed

of slaves who had belonged to the people he had proscribed and put to death. This bodyguard is said to have
numbered ten thousand men, and they were called
Cornelii, after Sulla's family name.

Under the rule of Sulla his own will was law. He could do
whatever he pleased. But he did not remain dictator a
long time. In about a year after his Triumph he seemed to
have got tired of ruling and resigned the office. Then he
left Rome and went to reside in his country house on the
beautiful Bay of Naples. Here he spent the rest of his life,
passing his time partly in feasting and merriment and
partly in study. He died 78 B.C.

POMPEY THE GREAT

I

Not long after the death of Sulla, a new enemy to Rome appeared upon the Mediterranean Sea. A large number of people who lived on the coasts of Asia Minor built and armed fleets of ships, sailed along the shores of Italy, and attacked and plundered Roman vessels.

The sea-rovers, or pirates, as the Romans called them, had more than a thousand well-built, fast-sailing ships. Many of them were adorned with richly gilded bows and sterns, purple sails, and silver-mounted oars. They seized trading-vessels, robbed them, and killed every person on board.

Often, too, the pirates committed robberies on land. A boat's crew from a pirate ship would go ashore, put to death all the farmers in the neighborhood, and lay waste their farms. So in a short time the pirates made themselves masters of the Italian coasts, and kept the people in constant excitement and terror.

But at last the Romans resolved to make war upon the robbers, and selected a very popular young man named Cne'i-us Pompey to be the general. The people had great confidence in Pompey. They said that he was the only one who could put down the Mediterranean pirates, and demanded that he should be sent to do the work.

Pompey was a fine-looking man, with very pleasant manners. He had made himself famous as a soldier by

brave deeds in wars in Spain and Africa, and was generally called Pompey the Great. His father had been a great
commander, and the boy had lived in camps and taken
part in wars almost from childhood. He had had many
adventures during his army life and had always shown the
qualities of a hero. He fought on the side of Sulla in many
battles against the Marians, and he was thought to be one
of Sulla's greatest generals.

The Roman Senate, therefore, yielded to the demand of
the people and appointed Pompey to go forth against the
pirates. He accepted the command and promptly set to
work to carry out the important undertaking.

He gathered fourteen powerful fleets. He kept one of
them for himself and put the others under the command
of good officers. Then he divided the Mediterranean into
thirteen districts, and sent a fleet to each district to hunt
the pirates.

With his own fleet he sailed as far as the Strait of
Gibraltar and then turned back towards Italy. On the way
he chased the pirate vessels before him as he met them,
until they were stopped and seized by some of the thirteen fleets stationed here and there all over the
Mediterranean. The pirates were thus caught in a trap.
Thousands of them were killed in battles with the different fleets, and their vessels were burned. The remainder
soon surrendered to the Romans, and in three months the
sea was cleared of pirates.

Pompey was much praised for this great work, and the
people said he was just the man to take charge of the war
against Mithridates. This king had again attacked a
Roman province in Asia, and the Romans resolved to
punish him. But Mithridates was a very powerful man. He
had great armies; he was a skillful general, and he defeated the Romans in many battles. The Roman people,
therefore, resolved to send Pompey against him. Pompey
was much pleased to be placed in command of a great
army, and he proudly started off with his soldiers for the
eastern lands.

II

Pompey remained in Asia several years and won many great victories. He conquered a number of countries and put Roman governors over them. Then he came back to Rome, bringing kings and princes as prisoners, and an enormous amount of gold and silver and other valuable things to enrich the Republic and himself. He was welcomed in a magnificent manner and he had a Triumph such as was given to great and victorious generals.

But Pompey now began to think of making himself master of Rome during his life-time. He had greatly pleased the people by his victories in war, and they were praising him on every side. How to keep their favor, and by it to get power was what now occupied his mind. He had been consul before, but he was now elected again, and then he set about providing various sorts of amusements for the people. He believed that if the people were amused they would be less likely to object to his taking the powers of the government entirely into his own hands.

He built a theatre large enough to seat forty thousand persons. This was the first great theatre erected in Rome. It was of stone and very strongly made. It had no roof, and the rows of seats rose one above another in a half circle. At one end there was an immense stage on which all the performances took place.

In this grand theatre Pompey gave some very wonderful exhibitions from time to time. He had lions, elephants, and other wild animals brought from Asia and Africa at a great expense. These animals were let loose upon the stage and gladiators fought them in full view of the people in the theatre.

There were also thrilling combats in the theatres between the gladiators themselves. They fought each other savagely until one was wounded and fell upon the stage. Then the victor would turn towards the audience to find whether they wished him to kill the wounded man. If the people wanted this they would stretch out their hands with the thumbs down; if they did not want him killed they would hold their thumbs upward. If he had shown skill and courage and fought well they would give the sign to let him live, but if he had not made a brave fight they would turn down their thumbs and the unfortunate man would be instantly killed.

Slaves and prisoners taken in war were taught to be gladiators in schools established for the purpose. There were hundreds of these trained fighters always ready for the combats. The Romans were very fond of such amusements, and great crowds of men, and women too, attended the theatre whenever there was a fight of gladiators.

By giving the people a great deal of amusement of this kind on a grand scale, Pompey became the great popular favorite in Rome, and while the people were entertained at his theatre he managed the government to suit himself.

III

At this time the Romans ruled a vast territory, which included not only all Italy, but Greece, Spain, Syria, Egypt, Turkey, Switzerland, and parts of France and Germany. Country after country had been conquered during a long series of years, and millions of people of different races and languages were subjects of Rome.

Rome itself was a city with a population of about half a million. It covered a very large area, including the famous seven hills. Its streets were narrow and crooked, but well-paved and clean. In the centre of the city were a number of large squares in which there were handsome buildings. There were magnificent temples and baths, and the houses of the nobles and wealthy plebeians were very large and splendid. Many of the fine houses were built of marble, with great pillars in front. Elegant furniture and handsome carpets and rugs filled the rooms.

There were many rich men in Rome at this time. Most of them had obtained the greater part of their wealth by plundering the conquered countries. They lived in a very magnificent manner, gave splendid dinners and entertainments, and had hundreds of slaves to attend upon them.

The slaves were a large class who were brought to Rome from many nations conquered in war. Many of them belonged to high families in their own country, and were well educated. Some of them were physicians, and others were good scholars and could read and write for their masters. The best cooks, builders, tailors, and farmers were slaves. In fact it was by slaves that nearly all the skilled work in Rome was done.

There were markets in Rome where slaves were sold. The slaves to be sold were placed on a platform. Labels hung from their necks, showing their age and what they were able to do.

The Roman children were taught to read and write Latin, which was their own language. They were also taught arithmetic and history. Most of the teachers were well-educated slaves.

Rome, then, was very rich and very powerful in the time of Pompey, and for many years Pompey was very popular. At one time he became dangerously ill while visiting Naples. Then the people showed their great love for him in many ways, and when he recovered there were public thanksgivings throughout Italy. On his journey home great crowds came out to greet him as he passed through the towns, and when he arrived at Rome he was received with unbounded joy.

Pompey had now a very strong hold on the affections of the people, so he cared little for the efforts made by a very ambitious Roman named Ju'li-us Cæ'sar to win public favor. But Cæsar was a man of strong will and great energy. He had resolved to be the ruler of Rome, and he spared no labor to accomplish his purpose. Pompey at last became alarmed at Cæsar's efforts, but it was then too late. He was defeated by Cæsar in a great battle and soon after lost his life. How these things came about we shall learn in the next story.

JULIUS CÆSAR

I

Of all the Roman heroes the greatest was Caius Julius Cæsar. He was a very remarkable man in many ways. He was remarkable as a soldier, statesman, scholar, and as an orator. He wrote a history of his own wars which is one of the best ancient histories that have come down to us. It is called *Cæsar's Commentaries*, and it is used as a text book in all schools where Latin is taught.

This famous Roman was tall, handsome, agreeable in his manners, and of a gay disposition. He liked songs and stories, and even when he was a great general he often was as merry and frolicsome as a boy. Sometimes, however, he was stern and cruel instead of kind and forgiving.

Cæsar was a member of the Julian family, which was one of the first families in Rome. Four Cæsars of this family had been consuls of Rome in one century.

The aunt of Julius Cæsar was the wife of the great leader, Marius. Naturally, Sulla was Cæsar's bitter enemy and did all he could against him. "In that young man there is many a Marius," Sulla is reported to have said. However, by keeping out of Rome, Cæsar was able to escape the traps laid for him at Sulla's orders. As soon as Sulla died Cæsar returned to Rome.

Although he was a rich noble, he became a friend of the plebeians and always supported their cause. He spoke a great deal in the Forum upon political questions, and the people looked upon him as their champion. They elected him to several public offices, one after the other, and thus his influence and power were much increased. At last he was appointed governor of Spain, which was then ruled by the Romans.

On his way to Spain he stopped for a night at a little village among the mountains. One of his companions remarked that perhaps in that small place the people had their contests and their jealousies, as well as people in large cities.

"Poor as this village is, I would rather be first here than second in Rome!" said Cæsar.

Cæsar was very successful in Spain, and the Romans were so pleased with his conduct that when he came home they made him consul. During his consulship he had many good laws passed. When about forty years old he was given command of an army, and for some years followed the life of a soldier with wonderful success.

The Roman armies were formed of regiments called *legions*. Each legion contained over three thousand men, who were sometimes called legionaries. The weapons of the legionary were a short sword and a long spear called a *pilum*.

Besides spears and swords the Roman soldiers used slings for hurling stones against the enemy. They also had a machine called a *ballista* for throwing stones too heavy for handslings.

The military standard of the Romans was a figure of an eagle borne on the top of a pole. Each legion had one of these and the soldier who carried it was called the *eagle-bearer*. Other standards also were used by the *cohorts* or companies into which the legions were divided.

Cæsar's first great battles were in Gaul. The Romans called all the inhabitants of that country Gauls, although they were of many nations and spoke different languages. The Gauls were brave, but Cæsar proved to be a great general, and in a few years he conquered all Gaul.

The Roman soldiers had great confidence in Cæsar. When he led them they believed victory was certain. He was strict in his discipline, but very friendly and pleasant with the men, and he often gave them praise. He himself shared in their hardships. Day after day he marched on foot at their head through heat and rain and snow, and fought with them in the front ranks.

On one occasion Cæsar built a very remarkable bridge. He wanted to get across the River Rhine with his army, to punish some German tribes who were in the habit of attacking the friends of Rome in Gaul. There was no bridge. The Germans used to get over in small parties by swimming, or in small boats. But a large army could not cross in this way without a great deal of trouble and loss of time, so Cæsar resolved to build a bridge. He quickly set his men to work and they finished the bridge in ten days, though all the wood had to be cut down in the forests and carried to the river side.

One of Cæsar's greatest victories in Gaul was the taking of the town of A-le'si-a. This town had very strong walls all round it and it was defended by a great army of Gauls commanded by a brave chief named Ver-cin-get'o-rix. Cæsar surrounded the town with his army and prevented food from being sent in to the inhabitants. He also defeated an army that came from other parts of Gaul to help the Alesians. Vercingetorix then had to come out from the town and give himself up to Cæsar.

After many conquests in Gaul Cæsar sailed over with an army to the island of Britain, now called Great Britain. The natives were a wild, fierce people, and they fought bravely against Cæsar and his army. But the Romans were victorious, and they took possession of Britain, and for over four hundred years the island was a part of the Roman Empire.

II

Cæsar was engaged eight years in his wars in Gaul and Britain. It is said that during these years he conquered three hundred tribes or nations, took eight hundred cities, fought battles with three millions of men and made a million prisoners. He obtained immense quantities of treasure in the conquered lands, and he himself, as commander of the victorious armies, kept a large part of it as his own share, so that he became very rich.

Cæsar's wonderful victories made him a great man in Rome. The plebeians rejoiced at the success of their leader and favorite and were ready to welcome him with the highest honors whenever he should return to the city.

But Cæsar had now made up his mind to become the master of Rome. So he began to plan and to work to destroy the power of Pompey, who at that time ruled public affairs in Rome almost completely.

In order to gain still greater favor Cæsar sent a number of his friends to Rome to spend immense sums of money in various ways to please the people. They got up splendid games and feasts; they divided large quantities of corn among the poor; and they paid the debts of hundreds of men who had influence among the plebeians. The people knew that all this was done at Cæsar's expense, and they praised and loved him for his generosity.

Pompey, with a great show of authority, now ordered Cæsar to disband his army and send the soldiers to their homes, for he said that Cæsar had no need of an army any longer, as he had finished his work in Gaul. But Pompey, too, had an army at this time in Spain, and Cæsar said to him:

"If you will disband your army, I will disband mine."

This made Pompey very angry, and he got the Senate to pass a law declaring that Cæsar was a public enemy and must be put down. One senator asked Pompey what he should do if Cæsar should come to Rome with his army.

"What should I do?" cried Pompey, in a tone of contempt. "Why, I have only to stamp my foot and thousands of men will spring up to march under my orders."

At that time Cæsar was with his army in the northern part of Italy. When he heard what the Senate had done he called his soldiers together and made an eloquent speech.

He told them of the injustice that Pompey and the Senate had done to him, and he concluded by saying:

"This is my reward for all that I have done for my country. But I shall go to Rome and establish an honest government of the people, if you, my brave soldiers, will be faithful to me."

The soldiers answered with a loud shout, saying:

"We shall be faithful to you. We will stand by you to the last."

Cæsar than started with his army and marched rapidly through northern Italy until he came to the banks of a little river, at that time called the Ru'bi-con, and known as the southern boundary of Gaul. What river this was no one can now exactly tell, but it is supposed that it was some one of several small rivers which flow into the Adriatic Sea south of the River Po.

Cæsar halted his army at the Rubicon and forbade any one to cross it until he gave the order. He stood for some time on the banks in deep thought, as if trying to decide whether he should cross the river and proceed, or give up his dangerous undertaking. He was still within his own territory as commander of Gaul; if he should cross the Rubicon he would be on territory directly under the government of the officers at Rome. By law it was made an act of treason, to be punished with death, for any Roman general to enter this territory with an army, without permission of the Senate.

"We can retreat now," said Cæsar to some of his officers who stood near him, "but once across the Rubicon it will be too late to draw back."

While Cæsar was talking a shepherd came along from a field close by, playing lively music on a reed pipe. The soldiers gathered around him to listen to the music, and some of them began to dance. One of Cæsar's trumpeters stood among the soldiers, with his trumpet in his hand. The shepherd saw the trumpet, suddenly seized it and walked to the bridge over the Rubicon, which was but a few steps off. Then he put the trumpet to his lips, sound-ed the stirring notes for an advance of the troops and began to march across the bridge.

"A sign from the gods!" shouted Cæsar. "Let us go where we are thus called. The die is cast!"

So saying, he turned his horse right into the stream and rode across the Rubicon, followed by his army. It was a daring thing even for Cæsar to do, and the phrases, "he has crossed the Rubicon," "the die is cast," are now often used to mean that a bold or dangerous step has been taken from which there is no drawing back.

There was no one to oppose Cæsar as he marched through Italy. On the contrary, city after city surrendered to him. There was very little fighting. In most places the people seemed glad to have him as their ruler, and gave him a warm welcome and feasted his soldiers. He had only words of kindness for every one, even for those who were against him, and he won hosts of friends and supporters all along his route.

There was great alarm at Rome when it was learned that Cæsar was advancing toward the city. The supporters of Pompey became terrified, and the rich nobles gathered up their money and other valuables and fled. Pompey could do nothing to defend the city against Cæsar, and at last he too ran away. He went to Greece to raise an army to fight Cæsar.

When Cæsar arrived at Rome he met with no opposition. He entered the city amid shouts of welcome from the people. He harmed no one, but he set up a new government and organized a new Senate. He was now the master spirit of the Republic.

After arranging everything to his satisfaction in Rome, he went to Spain and defeated Pompey's generals there. Then he came back and turned his attention to Pompey himself.

In the meantime Pompey had been very busy gathering an army in the eastern countries controlled by Rome. In one way and another he collected fifty thousand men. They were stationed on the coasts of Macedonia and

Greece. There they waited for Cæsar and his army to cross the Adriatic Sea to give them battle.

Cæsar had a great deal of trouble in getting across the stormy sea with his army of forty thousand soldiers, but at last a landing was made in Greece. Then the two armies had some skirmishing, but no great battle.

This continued for months. Pompey at one time would gain the advantage, and Cæsar at another time. But it was evident that neither of the great rivals was in any hurry to risk the chance of defeat in a general battle. They knew well that such a defeat would entirely ruin the one that was defeated.

But at last the two armies met for battle on the plain of Phar-sa'li-a, in Thessaly, a district of Greece. The soldiers on both sides were mostly armed with spears and broadswords. Some carried slings to hurl large stones, and others had bows and arrows. The greater part of the fighting, however, was done with swords.

Eighty thousand men were engaged in the battle, about forty thousand on each side. It was a brave, heroic struggle and lasted for hours. Both armies fought splendidly, but in the end Pompey's army was forced back to its camp, after dreadful slaughter. For a few minutes the camp was bravely defended against the attacks of Cæsar's soldiers and then had to be abandoned. The battle did not last long after this. Pompey's great army was utterly beaten.

Pompey himself, with a few followers, fled to the seashore and sailed across the Mediterranean to Egypt. There he was treacherously murdered by order of Ptolemy, the Egyptian king.

Cæsar gained a splendid victory at Pharsalia, but he was not yet master of the Roman Empire. The rich nobles and senators formed armies to fight him in Asia Minor, Africa, and Spain. Cæsar went with an army to Asia Minor, attacked his enemies, and won a great battle at a place called Ze'la. This victory was so quickly gained that in sending news of it to Rome Cæsar wrote the famous despatch, "*Veni, vidi, vici,*" which is, in English, "*I came, I saw, I conquered.*"

He had equal success in Africa and Spain. In a very short time he destroyed the armies opposed to him. Then he returned to Rome and had the grandest Triumph ever seen in the city.

The celebration lasted four days, and during that time Rome was in a high state of pleasant excitement. Thousands of persons from the surrounding country came to the city to witness the magnificent show.

On each day there were splendid processions, in which there were great numbers of gorgeous chariots, drawn by beautiful horses and filled with Cæsar's principal officers. Behind them marched hundreds of soldiers bearing banners on which were pictured scenes from Cæsar's important battles. Herds of elephants and camels from Asia and Africa appeared in the procession, and there were also long lines of prisoners carrying valuable articles obtained by Cæsar in the lands he had conquered.

In addition to the processions many kinds of entertainments were provided for the people, such as plays, circus exhibitions, combats between gladiators, wild-beast hunts, and chariot races. There were also feasts served to all the people of the city. It was a time of unbounded enjoyment and delighted the Romans so much that they became very devoted to Cæsar.

There was now no opposition to him. Both the nobles and the plebeians were willing, and even glad, to have him as their ruler. He was chosen dictator for life and put in command of all the armies of the Empire. He was called *imperator*, which means *emperor*.

The people gave him the title of *Father of his Country*. Statues of him were erected in the public buildings and squares. A grand chair, made somewhat like a throne, was placed in the Senate chamber, and whenever he came to listen to the debates he sat in this chair, as if he were king.

Cæsar now had laws passed making many improvements in the government. He also carried out a number of plans to make Rome of more importance as a commercial city. He erected magnificent buildings, made aqueducts to bring plenty of water to the city, established a great library, and did many other things which were of much benefit to the people.

One of the most useful things he did was to make a new calendar. Before his time the Romans had not a very clear knowledge as to the length of a year. At one time they had only ten months in their year. Afterwards they had twelve, but they counted only 365 days in every year. They did not know or they did not give attention to the fact that the real length of a year is 365 days, 5 hours, 48 minutes, 50 seconds. They did not reckon the extra hours, minutes, and seconds, and so their calendar got quite wrong in the course of a number of years. Cæsar corrected the error by making one year in every four have 366 days, and the calendar thus corrected was called the *Julian Calendar*.

Cæsar now possessed all the glory and power of a king, and it began to be believed that he wanted to be a king in reality. The Romans had not had a king for five hundred years and would not have one. Their feeling against kings was so strong that none of the men who had ruled Rome, at times with almost kingly power, had ever dared to call himself king.

One day an intimate friend of Cæsar saluted him in public as king. Cæsar replied:

"I am not king, but only Cæsar."

Some of the nobles, however, felt certain that he meant to make himself king, and they formed a plot to kill him in the Senate house, on the Ides of March, that is, on the fifteenth of March. The Romans had certain days in their months which they called Kalends, Nones, and Ides.

One of the persons who made the plot against Cæsar was Junius Brutus, a highly respected Roman. It is said that he was a descendant of the Junius Brutus who, five centuries before, had helped to overthrow the tyrant King Tarquin. Brutus was an intimate friend of Cæsar, but he thought that Cæsar intended to destroy the Republic by making himself king, and therefore he joined the plot against him.

As the Ides of March drew near the plan for putting Cæsar to death was carefully arranged and settled. An augur, or fortune-teller, one day stopped Cæsar in the street and said to him, "Beware the Ides of March!" but the great conqueror laughed at the warning.

On the appointed day the plotters met in the Senate chamber, ready to do the wicked deed they had planned. When Cæsar entered the chamber, all present rose to greet him. He bowed and smiled pleasantly to the people and took his usual seat. Now was the fatal moment.

As had been arranged, one of the plotters went up to him with a request for the pardon of a prisoner. Then the rest crowded around his chair, as if to urge him to grant the request. Cæsar seemed somewhat alarmed at the crowd and rose from his chair. At this moment he was stabbed in the side with a sword. Then there were loud outcries in the chamber, and all was excitement and confusion.

Cæsar used his stylus to defend himself. The stylus was an instrument made of iron, with a sharp point on one end for writing on wax tablets, and with the other end smooth, for rubbing out a word when necessary. For writing on parchment or paper a pen made of reed was used. Educated Romans carried their stylus and tablet in their pockets. From the name of the instrument the word *style* is now used to mean a particular manner of writing.

Cæsar had nothing but his stylus to defend himself with. He fought bravely, until he saw his friend Brutus coming to strike him. Then he cried out, "You, too, Brutus!" and made no further resistance.

They stabbed him until he fell dead. Then they went out of the Senate and through the streets of Rome with Brutus at their head. They told the people what they had done and rejoiced at the deed. They said the death of Cæsar saved the Roman Republic.

But the people were very angry and threatened to put

to death those who had killed Cæsar. They would have done this only that Brutus and his friends fled from the city.

There was a grand funeral service in honor of Cæsar. The body was laid in the Forum, and a famous Roman named Mark Antony made an eloquent funeral speech over it. He praised Cæsar and spoke so bitterly against Brutus and his party that the people were more angry than ever. This Mark Antony was afterwards a very powerful man in Rome.

Cæsar died forty-four years before Christ was born. Of course his death did not save the Roman Republic. It had, indeed, already ceased to exist in all but the name. Rome was no longer a republic, but an Empire and, as we shall see, the family of Cæsar gave it its first emperor. All the emperors adopted the name of Cæsar as part of their title.

CICERO

I

Marcus Tul'li-us Cic'e-ro was a prominent man at Rome for some time in the latter years of the Republic. He was a great orator—one of the greatest the world has ever known. His principal speeches have been preserved and are read and studied at the present day.

He often spoke in the Forum before large audiences, and by his wonderful eloquence delighted all who heard him. Both the nobles and plebeians admired him for his learning, his oratory, and his manly qualities.

Cicero was a tall, graceful man, with an intellectual and rather handsome face, and very bright, black eyes. He was so great a favorite that he was chosen to fill several public offices and at last was elected consul.

In the early part of his year as consul there was a mysterious plot formed in Rome by some nobles of bad character, old soldiers, and others ready for any mischief. What their real object was no one seemed to know. But it was said that the conspirators wanted to overthrow the government and set up a new one of their own.

There was a senator named Ser'gi-us Cat'i-line, and many believed that he was at the head of the plot. He had a bad reputation, and for some time the other senators had looked upon him with suspicion. There was no proof, however, that he was engaged in any unlawful proceedings, so no charge could be made against him.

But one day a young woman, named Fulvia, came to

115

Cicero and gave him some important information about
the plot and Catiline's part in it. She said that she had a
lover who was one of the plotters, and that he had told
her some of their secrets. She was greatly frightened, for
she thought that there might be bloodshed in Rome if the
plot went on, and she felt it her duty to tell Cicero about
it.

Cicero immediately went to the Senate and made a powerful speech. He charged Catiline with being the leading
person in a plot to overthrow the government. There was
great excitement at his words. Catiline was present, and
he boldly denied the charge and defied Cicero to prove it.

"If Consul Cicero is afraid of my doing harm in Rome,"
said he, "I am willing to place myself as a prisoner in the
hands of any senator."

"I do not think it is safe to have you in the city," replied
Cicero, "and do you expect any one to take you into his
house?"

After a great deal of exciting talk the Senate laid aside
the charges against Catiline for a while.

II

A few weeks later, in a city near Rome, there was an upris-
ing of the people against the public officers. This caused
a great deal of alarm, and Cicero said it was the beginning
of the plot that he had charged Catiline with forming.

Then he hurried to the Senate, where Catiline was, and
made a great speech against him. He called him a traitor
to his country. Catiline turned pale and began to tremble.
He attempted to speak, but the senators shouted, and
hooted and hissed him. Those who sat near him got up in
disgust and took seats in another part of the chamber,
leaving the conspirator sitting by himself. At last Catiline
ran out of the Senate, furious with anger, and threatening
revenge. Then he mounted a horse and rode quickly out
of the city.

Shortly afterwards Cicero learned the names of nine

Roman citizens who were leaders in the plot, and he had them arrested. He declared in the Senate that they had planned to murder the senators and the high officers, and to burn Rome. The senators declared at once that the nine must die, and so Cicero had them put to death.

Catiline now fled to the mountains called the Apennines and there raised a force of twenty thousand men. Two armies were sent against him from Rome. A battle took place, in which Catiline's army was defeated and he himself killed.

Thus ended what was known as the Catiline Conspiracy. Cicero's action in helping to destroy it greatly pleased the Romans. In the Senate he received much praise and honor. It was even declared that he was the "Father of his Country."

Antony did not like Cicero, and when the Triumvirate was formed, the great orator was put to death by Antony's order.

AUGUSTUS

I

The first of the long line of Roman emperors was Oc-ta'vi-us, called in history Au-gus'tus. He was the grandnephew of Julius Cæsar. Although he was scarcely twenty years old when Cæsar died, he was very ambitious. He often said that he should one day be at the head of the Roman Empire.

"I shall rule Rome like Cæsar," he would say to his companions. "You may laugh at me now, but the time will come when I shall be master of the Romans."

Shortly after Cæsar's death Octavius began to take an active part in political affairs. At this time Mark Antony was in control of Rome and was managing everything to suit himself. He had been an intimate friend of Cæsar and commanded one of his armies. He obtained a great deal of power, but he was not liked very much either by the nobles or the plebeians. He was a bad ruler, and nobody trusted him.

Once Antony tried to prevent Octavius from being elected a tribune of the people. "I will be a tribune in spite of you," Octavius said, and he set to work with all his energy to get the office. There was a severe struggle on election day, but the boy was successful.

After this Octavius hated Antony and planned in secret to bring about his downfall. And he succeeded in all he attempted to do. From a tribune he advanced steadily, step by step, to more important offices. At last he obtained command of an army and marched his soldiers to northern Italy, where a war was going on. While in this region he met Antony with his army. The two began to quarrel and at last came to blows. Then the army of Octavius fought the army of Antony, and the northern plains were reddened with the blood of the soldiers.

When the fighting had gone on for some time, Octavius sent to Antony and asked him to stop it. He pretended that he was very sorry he had begun to fight with Antony and asked for his friendship.

"Let us be friends and work together," he said to Antony. "By joining our armies we shall be able to do some good."

The fighting was then stopped, and the two generals had a meeting. They agreed to unite their armies, and to invite another Roman general, named Lep'i-dus, who had a large army, to join them. Lepidus accepted the invitation and came to have a talk with Antony and Octavius. They agreed to a plan by which they themselves were to rule Rome together. This rule, or government, was called a *triumvirate*, and Octavius, Antony, and Lepidus were called *triumvirs*, a word which means *three men*.

II

After making all their arrangements, Antony, Octavius, and Lepidus started for Rome with their armies and took possession of the city. Then they began to kill those that they thought were their enemies. More than two thousand Romans were slain. They would have killed Brutus only that he was then in Greece, where he had gone after Cæsar's death to raise an army to fight Antony and his friends. Antony and Octavius now went with an army to Greece to fight Brutus. Both armies met at Philippi, in Macedonia, and then there was a battle in which the army of Brutus was defeated. After the battle Brutus requested one of his slaves to kill him. The slave refused, but when Brutus still pressed him to do it, he held out his sword and Brutus killed himself by falling upon it.

It is told that some time before the battle of Philippi, as Brutus was sitting one night in his tent, a vision or spectre appeared to him and said, "I am thy evil genius, Brutus; we shall meet again at Philippi." It is also said that the spectre again appeared to Brutus on the night before the battle of Philippi and told him that his death was at hand.

There was no one now to interfere with Antony, Octavius, and Lepidus, and they managed everything in Rome as they liked. They pretended all the time to have great respect for the Senate and the officers of government who had been elected by the people.

After a short time Antony went to some of the Eastern countries that were a part of the Roman Empire, and Lepidus went to Africa. Octavius was left in Rome to attend to its affairs. He then began to plan to get rid of Antony and Lepidus, so that he might rule Rome himself. With this object he raised a great army and determined to make war on his rivals.

Sextus Pompey, a son of Pompey the Great, was at this time in control of the island of Sicily. He was always making trouble for Octavius, and he was aided by Lepidus, who had come from Africa to Sicily with his army. One day Octavius sailed over the Mediterranean Sea to Sicily, with thousands of soldiers, destroyed the army of Sextus, and induced the army of Lepidus to leave him. Lepidus was then taken prisoner.

"Now to put an end to the power of Antony!" said Octavius to himself, when he returned to Rome from Sicily. So he went to the Senate and accused Antony of treason in Asia and Africa and asked that war be declared against him. The Senate declared war, and Octavius began to make great preparations for it.

Antony was in Egypt when he heard of the declaration of war. He laughed scornfully at the idea of Octavius being able to beat him. Then he gathered an army of more than a hundred thousand men and a fleet of several hundred

warships, and set out to meet Octavius. He had with him
Cle-o-pa'tra, the beautiful queen of Egypt, whom he had
married, and she had a fleet of her own, numbering sixty
ships.

Octavius had about as many soldiers and ships as
Antony. The two fleets met near a place called Ac'ti-um,
on the coast of Greece, and fought a battle. For several
hours the fight went on bravely, but neither side gained
any great advantage. Suddenly Cleopatra sailed away with
her fleet, and Antony quickly followed her with a few
ships. Thus he deserted his men while they were fighting.

The sailors and soldiers of the deserted fleet kept on
fighting for a short time and then surrendered
to Octavius. A few days later a part of Antony's army,
which was encamped on the shore near Actium, also
surrendered.

Antony went back to Egypt with Cleopatra. His friends
and supporters then left him, and his power was gone.
Soon after, he stabbed himself, and so died. It is said that
Cleopatra died from the bite of a poisonous serpent called
an asp, which she placed on her arm on purpose to kill
herself.

III

Octavius continued to fight in different parts of the
Empire until he defeated every one who dared to oppose
him. Then he went back to Rome with a great deal of glory
and riches and let it be known at once that he intended to
be the master of the government. Although he pretended
to protect the rights of the people, he made himself consul and also assumed other high offices which greatly
added to his power. Thousands of soldiers were at his
call, and finally he became very much like a king.

The Senate asked him if he would wish to be appointed
dictator for life, but he thought it wise to refuse this office.
The Senate then gave him the name of Augustus, which
meant that he was worthy of respect. The word *augustus*

in the Latin language means *sacred*. He called himself emperor, and, as Emperor Cæsar Augustus, he ruled the Romans all the rest of his life, a period of about twenty-seven years. And when Augustus became emperor the Republic of Rome was no longer in existence.

What were known as the Præ-to'ri-an Guards were organized by Augustus to protect himself and uphold his authority as emperor. These guards were about ten thousand in number, and they were composed of the most trusty soldiers of the Empire. Each soldier had high rank and large pay, and had to serve for many years. Whenever Augustus appeared in public he was attended by some of the Prætorian Guards, and they looked very imposing with their handsome uniforms and glittering swords and spears.

Augustus made many good changes in the government. He very much improved the condition of the plebeians. His principal ministers were two able men named A-grip'-pa and Mæ-ce'nas, who gave him very valuable assistance.

Whenever these wise men saw that the Romans were getting uneasy and beginning to grumble, they would advise the emperor to distribute corn or money to the poor, or to give the people grand exhibitions to amuse them. Augustus would follow the advice, and by so doing made himself very popular.

During his long reign Augustus had many splendid palaces, temples, and other buildings erected in Rome, and they made the city very beautiful. Augustus also founded cities in various parts of the Empire. He encouraged literature and art and was himself an author. In his time the famous Roman poets, Hor'ace, Ver'gil, Va'ri-us, and Ovid lived, and also the great historian Livy, who wrote the history of Rome from the earliest period down to his own time. Vergil was the author of a celebrated poem called the *Æ-ne'id*, which tells of the wanderings and adventures of the Trojan hero Æneas mentioned on page 1 of this book.

It was in the reign of Augustus that Jesus Christ was born in Bethlehem, a town of Palestine, or Judea, in Southwest Asia. Judea was then part of the Roman Empire.

NERO

I

On the death of Augustus in the year 14 A.D. his stepson Ti-be'ri-us became emperor. He was a cruel tyrant. He put to death a great many people only because he thought they were his enemies. A Roman emperor could put to death any one he pleased. If he did not like a person, he would charge him with some crime and order his soldiers to kill him. Tiberius had many people killed in this way, but he was himself killed by the commander or general of the Prætorian Guard.

The next two emperors were Ca-lig'u-la and Clau'di-us. They also were tyrants and put many people to death without just cause. It is said that Caligula once wished that all the Roman people together had but one head so that he might cut it off with one blow.

But the next emperor was a still greater tyrant. His name was Nero. He became emperor in the year 54 A.D. He was the son of a wicked woman named Ag-rip-pi'na. This woman married the Emperor Claudius and got him to appoint her son, Nero, his successor, instead of his own little son, Bri-tan'ni-cus. Then she killed Claudius by poison, and Nero became emperor.

Nero was a tall, strong, good-looking, bright youth. He was fond of games, and could play well on several musical insruments. When he first became emperor he seemed to be affectionate and kind-hearted, and he did a number of good things. Once, when he was asked to sign a warrant for the execution of a man condemned to death, he exclaimed:

"I wish I had never learned to write, for then I shouldn't have to sign away men's lives!"

Then all the people around him cried:

"What a noble young man our emperor is! What a good heart he has!"

But in a very short time it was found that Nero was not at all kind or merciful, but that he was a cruel and wicked man.

His mother Agrippina expected that when her son was emperor she herself would be the real mistress and would rule the Roman Empire as she pleased. Nero was only a boy, she thought, and he would not want to take upon himself the cares and burdens of government.

And for a while Agrippina did rule Rome. She had a woman she hated put to death and she punished several other persons who had offended her. She made some of the richest Romans pay her large sums of money. But Nero soon put an end to his mother's power. One day he said to her:

"I, not you, am the ruler of the Empire. You have no right to take any power upon yourself and you must not do so again. Whenever you want anything done you must ask me to do it for you."

"Ask you?" cried Agrippina, in a rage. "How dare you talk this way to me who made you emperor? You the emperor! You are not the rightful emperor. The true heir to the Empire is your stepbrother, young Britannicus, the son of Claudius!"

Then there was a fierce quarrel between Nero and his mother, and at last he turned her out of his palace and ordered her never to appear there again.

But what she had said alarmed him very much. He feared that Britannicus might be made emperor, and therefore he determined to get him out of the way as soon as possible.

At this time there was in Rome a dreadful woman

named Lo-cus'ta, who made poisons and sold them secretly to any one who wanted them. Nero went one night to this woman and said:

"Make me a strong poison—so strong that it will kill a person like a flash of lightning!"

Locusta made the poison and gave it to him. He tried it on a pig, and it killed the animal in a few moments.

"Ha!" said he, "this will do the work."

Now, Britannicus lived in the palace with his stepbrother and next day, when dinner was served, Nero put some of the poison into a cup of wine which he knew the boy was to drink. The moment Britannicus drank it, he fell to the floor dead. Then Nero said to the guests who were at the table:

"Do not be alarmed. It is nothing. My poor stepbrother always was subject to fits."

The attendants carried the body of Britannicus out of the room, and the dinner went on gayly.

II

A little while after he had poisoned his stepbrother, Nero made up his mind to get rid of his mother, also. He was afraid that as long as she lived he would not be safe as emperor. She might stir up the people against him any day. So he went to see her and pretended that he was sorry he had ill-treated her. He kissed and caressed her so affectionately that she was entirely deceived.

Then the cruel son made a plan to drown his mother. He had a ship so built that by pulling out certain bolts and pins it would suddenly fall to pieces and sink. He then hired a wicked captain and crew to do his bidding, and got his mother to take a sail in the ship down the Tiber.

Agrippina took a maid with her and went aboard. She was in a happy humor, because her son, as she thought, was so kind to her. When the ship came to a certain place in the river where the water was very deep, the sailors pulled out the bolts and pins. Then the ship began to fall apart and to sink.

The sailors sprang into the river to swim to the shore, and Agrippina and her maid jumped overboard. The maid was killed by a sailor, but Agrippina was picked up by the crew of a fishing boat.

Nero was greatly troubled when he learned of his mother's escape. He believed that now she would certainly try to have him removed from the throne. So he sent some men to kill her in her house, and they did so in a most cruel manner.

III

None of the emperors before Nero lived so grandly as he did. He had a splendid marble palace at Rome, containing immense quantities of beautiful furniture, gold and silver ornaments, and works of art of the finest kind. On the pleasant shores of the Mediterranean Sea he had several houses where he lived in the summer and autumn months. Wherever he went he had, as his court or companions, three or four hundred richly dressed men and women, with many slaves to wait upon them. They traveled in chariots covered with ivory and gold and drawn by beautiful horses.

Nero was famous for the splendid dinners he gave in his palace. The rarest and most costly food and wines were spread upon the tables in great plenty, and when the feasting was over troops of actors and dancers would give performances which lasted until late at night.

Sometimes, at these dinners, Nero would play on a harp or flute, and sometimes he would act portions of plays or recite poems which he himself had composed. He was a very clever musician and actor, and he wrote very good poetry.

One evening a fire broke out in Rome and raged furiously for a week. Half the city was burned, and hundreds of people lost their lives. Some of the Romans said that

Nero had started the fire and had prevented it from being put out. Most of the six days during which the fire lasted he spent in a high tower, enjoying the sight. He played on his harp, sang merry songs, and recited verses about the burning of the ancient city of Troy.

After the fire was put out Nero said that it had been caused by the believers in the religion of Christ. At this time there was a very large number of Christians in Rome. But most of the Romans still worshiped their old pagan gods, and they hated and ill-treated the Christians.

When Nero declared that the Christians had caused the great fire, the people began to persecute them in a dreadful manner. Many of the Christians were hanged, some were covered with pitch and burned, and others were hunted to death by savage dogs. During the time of this persecution the Apostle Paul was beheaded and the Apostle Peter was crucified, as Christ had been crucified thirty-one years before.

After a short time Rome was rebuilt in a greater magnificence than before. Nero built for himself an immense and splendid palace on the famous Palatine Hill. This palace contained so many ornaments of gold that it was called the Golden House.

In governing the Empire Nero was very harsh and cruel. He often put innocent men and women, and even his own friends, to death. He killed his wife in a fit of passion. He did so many wicked things that at last the Romans got tired of having such a tyrant to rule them, and they formed a plot to dethrone him and make some one else their emperor.

But the plot came to nothing, because a slave who had heard of it went to Nero and told him all about it. The Prætorian Guards seized the leading plotters and put them to death. Nero then became more wicked than he had been before. He even accused his old tutor Seneca, and the famous poet Lucan, of taking part in the plot against him, and he sent them an order to put themselves to death. Seneca was a very good man and a great writer.

When he received the cruel order from Nero, he knew that if he did not obey it the tyrant would send some one to kill him, so he had the veins of his arms cut open and he died after much suffering. Lucan also obeyed the tyrant's order. While dying he repeated lines from one of his own poems.

IV

This wicked emperor reigned fourteen years. But at last there was a rebellion against him, and the soldiers elected Galba, the Roman governor of Spain, to be the new emperor.

Then Nero acted like a miserable coward. He was afraid to stay any longer in Rome, for most of the people hated him and favored Galba. So he mounted a horse and rode out of the city to the home of a trusty slave. But while he was there he received word that the Senate had condemned him to death and that horsemen had been sent out to capture him.

"Now dig a grave for me," he said to the slave, "and I will kill myself!"

At this moment the galloping of horses was heard.

"Hark! They are coming to kill you," cried the slave. "Use the dagger while it is time and save yourself from disgrace!"

With trembling hand Nero placed his dagger at his throat, but did not have the courage to use it. The slave then seized it and plunged it into the emperor's throat, and the wicked Nero fell dead.

TITUS

I

During the two years that followed the death of Nero, there were three emperors, Galba, Otho, and Vi-tel'li-us. They were generals of Roman armies, and were made emperors by their soldiers. But they reigned only a few months each, and they did nothing of importance.

Vitellius was a glutton. He took pleasure only in eating and drinking. He would often visit the houses of rich Romans without invitation and take breakfast with one, dinner with another, and supper with another. After breakfast he thought only about dinner; and when dinner was over he began to think of what he would have for supper.

The next emperor was Titus Flavius Vespasian, commonly called Vespasian. He also was an army general. When he was made emperor by his soldiers he was in Palestine. He had been sent there by Nero with an army to punish the Jews who had rebelled against Rome. As soon as he was declared emperor he returned to Italy and left his son Titus Flavius, called in history simply Titus, to carry on the war against the Jews.

Titus captured Jerusalem after a siege of six months, and his soldiers took possession of all the valuable things they could find. Then they burned the city to the ground. The famous temple was also destroyed, and thus was fulfilled the prophecy of Christ that not one stone of the building should be left upon another. When Titus returned to Rome he had a grand Triumph, and a beautiful arch was built in his honor. This arch is still in existence.

II

Vespasian died in 79 A.D., and then Titus became emperor. One of the remarkable things Titus did during his reign was to finish the Colosseum, which had been begun by his father.

The Colosseum was the largest theatre in the world. It had seats for over 80,000 people. It was first called the Flavian Amphitheatre, from the family name of the emperors who built it. Inside it had seats all round the ring, or arena, and as the word *amphi* means *around*, they called the great building an amphitheatre. In later times it got the name of Colosseum. The Greeks used the word *colossus* as a name for any very large statue, and because the Flavian Amphitheatre was so large it was called the Colosseum. In our own language we use the word *colossal* to describe anything of immense size.

In the Colosseum they had many kinds of amusements. When it was first opened the shows and games lasted for a hundred days, and 5,000 wild beasts were killed in the arena by gladiators. The arena was a vast space fenced round about with a strong wall, and around it were circular tiers or rows of seats, one behind the other, like steps of stairs. Sometimes the arena was turned into a lake by letting water flow into it from pipes. Then they put ships upon it and had sham fights in imitation of a battle at sea. This sort of show was called *naumachia*, which means a fight with ships. It was first introduced into Rome by Julius Cæsar, who had a lake dug for the purpose in the Campus Martius.

The Colosseum is still in existence, but it is partly in ruins.

Besides finishing the Colosseum, the Emperor Titus also built splendid baths. They were called the Baths of Titus. The Romans were very fond of baths. Wealthy citizens used to bathe several times every day, and often they spent the greater part of the day at the baths, where there were finely furnished rooms.

It was in the reign of Titus that the cities of Pom-pe'ii (-pā'yi) and Hercu-la'ne-um, in the south of Italy, were destroyed by an eruption of Mount Vesuvius. A famous Roman author, Pliny the Younger, saw the eruption from a distance and wrote a description of it. He tells that a fiery cloud of cinders, stones, and ashes burst from the top of the mountain and rained down upon the country all round, destroying towns and villages and people. The ruins of Herculaneum were accidentally discovered by workmen in 1709, and the ruins of Pompeii were discovered some years later.

Titus was a very good emperor. He always did everything he could for the welfare and happiness of the people, and he was so much liked by everybody that he was called the "Delight of Mankind." It is said that one night he thought he had done nothing during that day for the good of any person, and that he cried out, "I have lost a day."

TRAJAN

I

On the death of Titus his brother Domitian became emperor. He was a very bad man and took pleasure only in doing cruel and wicked things. It is said that one of his amusements was catching flies and sticking them with pins. Once when a visitor called and inquired whether there was any one with the emperor, the servant answered, "No, not even a fly."

It is not to be supposed that such an emperor could have been liked by the people. Even his soldiers hated him, and at last they formed a plot against his life and killed him in his own palace.

Nerva, who had been a favorite of Nero, was the next emperor, but he was an old man and died after a reign of two years. He was succeeded by his adopted son Trajan, who became emperor in 98 A.D. and reigned for nineteen years.

Trajan was a good man and a brave soldier. At the time he became emperor he was governor of one of the Roman territories or provinces in Germany along the banks of the Rhine, and he resided at Colonia, now called Cologne.

Not long after his return to Rome Trajan was engaged in a war with the King of Dacia. This was the name of the country lying north of the Danube River. The greater part of it is now called Hungary. The Dacian king, whose name was De-ceb'a-lus, had frequently made raids into neighboring countries which belonged to Rome, and robbed and killed many of the people. Trajan resolved to punish Decebalus, and so he set out with a large army and marched into Dacia. The war continued three years, for the Dacians were brave and skillful fighters; but at last Decebalus was defeated in a great battle and he had to come to Trajan and humbly beg for peace. He agreed to be a vassal of Rome; that is, to hold his kingdom subject to the control of the Roman emperors.

But in less than a year Decebalus again attacked his Roman neighbors, and Trajan had again to march against him with an army. The Dacians were once more defeated in a great battle, and Decebalus, after failing in an attempt to escape, put an end to his own life. Dacia was then made a Roman province.

During this year Trajan built a remarkable bridge across the Danube. Before that time bridges were built of wood, but in the bridge over the Danube Trajan used stone for the piers, which were of great size. The bridge had twenty-two arches, and its ruins, which are still to be seen, show what a wonderful work it was.

When Trajan returned to Rome after his victory over Decebalus he had a grand Triumph, and there were games and shows in his honor which lasted a hundred and twenty days. It is told that during these celebrations 10,000 gladiators fought in the amphitheatre and 11,000 wild animals were killed in the arena.

A marble column was erected in honor of Trajan's victories in Dacia. This monument is still standing in Rome. It is called Trajan's Column. Many scenes showing battles and other events in the Dacian war are engraved upon it from the base to the top.

II

Trajan also had wars in Asia, and he won many victories. He conquered Armenia and Mesopotamia and added them to the Empire. But he did not live to return to Rome. He died in a town in Asia Minor, which in honor of him was afterwards called Trajanopolis.

The Romans were much grieved at the death of Trajan, for he had been a good emperor and had done much to benefit the people. He built fine roads and canals and bridges in Italy and the provinces. He greatly improved and beautified the Circus Maximus. This was the place in which the Romans had their horse races and chariot races. It was built in the hollow between the Palatine and Aventine hills, and it had seats for 250,000 people.

Trajan also made a forum in Rome, which was called after his name the Trajan Forum. In the centre of this forum the Trajan Column was built, and around it were temples and libraries established by the good emperor. For a long time after Trajan's death the people of Rome, whenever they got a new emperor, used to wish that he would be "as great as Augustus and as good as Trajan."

Some great writers lived in Rome in the time of Trajan. One of them was Plutarch, who wrote the famous book called *Plutarch's Lives*. This book, which you will perhaps some day read, contains an account of the lives of many great men of Greece and Rome. The historian Tacitus, the poet Juvenal, and Pliny the Younger, already mentioned, also lived in the time of Trajan.

Pliny the Younger was so-called to distinguish him from his uncle, Pliny the Elder, who lived in the time of Nero and was the author of a celebrated work on natural history.

MARCUS AURELIUS

I

The next emperor was Trajan's cousin Ha'dri-an. He was a good ruler and did a great deal to improve the city of Rome. He traveled through many parts of the Empire to see that the people were justly governed and that the public officials were doing their duty. He visited Britain, which was then a Roman province, and he caused a strong wall to be built from sea to sea across the country near Scotland, to prevent the fierce tribes of the north from making raids upon the Roman settlements in the south. Some of the remains of this wall are still to be seen.

Hadrian also built a great tomb in Rome, which was called Hadrian's Mole. He and many other Roman emperors were buried in this tomb. It is now known as the Castle of St. Angelo.

When Hadrian died a very good man named An-to-ni'nus was made emperor. He showed such filial regard for Hadrian, by building a temple in his honor, that he was called Antoninus Pi'us. Under the emperors who ruled before his time the Christians were very cruelly treated. They were not allowed to have churches or places of worship, and numbers of them were put to death in the most shocking manner. Often Christians were thrown into the arena in the Amphitheatre and devoured by wild beasts.

In those times the Christians of Rome held their religious meetings in underground passages dug for burying places. These Catacombs, as they were called, were near the walls of the city and altogether were hundreds of miles in length. Along both sides of the tunnels were openings, one above another, in which the dead were buried. Many of the Catacombs have been explored in recent times. They are among the "sights" which visitors to Rome are always eager to see.

Antoninus Pius was very friendly to the Christians. He gave orders that they should be allowed to practice their religion and that any one who interfered with them should be punished.

The next emperor of Rome was a very remarkable and a very good man. His name was Mar'cus Au-re'li-us. He governed the Empire justly and well for nearly twenty years. He began to reign in the year 161 A.D. He was the adopted son of the good Emperor Antoninus. For some time before the death of Antoninus, he held a high office and helped to govern the Empire.

As soon as he became emperor Aurelius invited a young man named Ve'rus to share the throne with him. Verus had also been adopted by Antoninus. The generous act of Aurelius surprised everybody. Never before was there a Roman emperor who wanted to give half of his power to another person, and it seemed strange to the people that Aurelius should do so. But Aurelius said:

"I think my adopted brother has a right to be emperor with me."

And so Verus was made emperor with Aurelius, and for the first time Rome was ruled by two emperors. Verus had a great respect for Aurelius. He seldom attempted to do anything in matters of government without asking his advice. But he did not have much to do with public affairs. He cared very little about being emperor and generally spent his time in amusing himself. He was not a good young man, and his conduct gave Aurelius a great deal of sorrow. But after nine years Verus died, and Aurelius was the sole ruler during the rest of his life.

In his youth Aurelius studied under the best teachers in the Empire, and so had an excellent education. He always had an eager desire for knowledge and was constantly learning. Even in war times, when he was fighting in the field, he carried a library with him and could often be seen in his tent engaged in study. He was one of the most learned of the Roman emperors, and his intimate friends were scholars and authors.

When a boy of only twelve years he joined the Sto'ics. These were followers of a famous wise man or philosopher of Greece, called Ze'no. This man taught that the people should act according to reason and virtue, and should keep an even temper and a brave heart under all circumstances. He taught also that men should show neither joy nor sorrow, but control their feelings and passions, and submit without complaint to what could not be prevented.

The followers of Zeno were called Stoics, from the Greek word *stoa*, which means a roofed colonnade or porch. It was in a roofed porch at Athens that Zeno taught his doctrine.

The Emperor Aurelius was one of the best and most earnest of the Stoics. He carefully trained himself to control his feelings at all times and to do his duty honestly and faithfully. The Romans never had a purer or nobler emperor, or one more respected and beloved. His style of living was very simple. He had no idle courtiers at his house, and he kept only a few servants. He gave no costly dinners and entertainments. He spent much of his salary to improve the condition of the poor and to provide good schools for their children.

He used to walk through the streets of Rome in plain clothing, attended only by a favorite slave. He returned the greetings of the people with bows and pleasant smiles. Any one could go to him and talk freely, and he encouraged the people to tell him about their troubles so that he might understand how to help them.

He gave the Senate a great deal of power which he thought it ought to have, and gave back to the people many rights and privileges which former emperors had

taken away from them. No wonder the Romans loved him
and called him a good man.

II

But the reign of Aurelius was full of troubles. In the first
part of it the Tiber one day overflowed its banks, and the
waters swept away a large portion of Rome, destroying
many lives. After this there were dreadful earthquakes,
very destructive fires, and other serious misfortunes.

There were also many wars. There was a war with the
Parthians, a brave, warlike nation in Asia, who destroyed
a Roman army and then invaded Syria. Large armies were
sent against them and they were soon conquered and
forced to pay homage to Aurelius.

The Parthian horsemen had a strange way of fighting.
They were armed with bows and arrows and small spears
called javelins, and were mounted on very swift horses.
They would make attacks on the rear lines of the Romans,
and when the Romans turned to attack them they would
lash their horses and ride off as fast as the wind. And
while their horses were going at full speed they would
turn in their saddles and cast their javelins, or shoot their
arrows with wonderfully accurate aim.

After the Parthian war there were wars with a number
of wild tribes living in the countries now called Austria
and Hungary. The tribes there rebelled against their
Roman governors, and Aurelius had years of hard fighting
before he could subdue them. He was himself a remarkably brave and able general and gained many splendid
victories. So at last he taught the barbarians to respect
and obey the Romans who governed them.

Once, while Aurelius was fighting a tribe called the
Qua'di, his soldiers were hemmed in by the enemy, in a
small rocky valley, and suffered greatly from thirst.
Suddenly the sky darkened and rain fell in torrents. The
thirsty soldiers collected the water in their helmets and
drank it eagerly.

While they were drinking, and their lines were in confusion, the Quadi suddenly attacked them in large numbers. The Romans would have been cut to pieces but that there came a violent hailstorm, with lightning and thunder, which stopped the battle. When the storm had ceased, the Romans, much refreshed by the rainfall, boldly fought the Quadi and won a great victory.

Some of the Romans believed that the sudden storm which relieved them so much was caused by the magical power of an African wizard who was with the army at the time. But there was also with the army a legion of soldiers, some 3,000 in number, who were Christians. The Christians had prayed for rain, and they believed that the rain came in answer to their prayers. They said that it was a miracle sent by God to prove the truth of Christianity.

Now Aurelius was a pagan. Some of his Christian soldiers had tried to convert him to their faith, but they had not succeeded. He lived and died a believer in the pagan gods and goddesses. After the strange storm, however, he seemed to have a greater respect for Christianity, and he named his Christian legion of soldiers the "Thundering Legion."

III

Once the commander of the Roman armies in Asia, a man named A-vi'di-us Cas'si-us, planned a rebellion against Aurelius. When everything was ready Cassius declared himself emperor and started with his army to Rome to take possession of the city. Aurelius collected his troops and went to meet Cassius; but no meeting took place, for Cassius was killed by his own soldiers, and the rebellion quickly came to an end.

Those who had aided Cassius were brought before Aurelius for punishment. But the emperor would not punish them.

"No, I will not harm them," he said. "I think I have governed the Empire too faithfully and liberally to fear plots.

I can afford to forgive traitors. Let all the friends of Cassius go free; they are to be pitied rather than punished."

Aurelius was always very industrious and would never waste any of his time. It was a part of his duty as emperor to attend the games and sports in the Colosseum and the Circus. Aurelius cared nothing for such sports and whenever he attended them, he always spent his time at some useful occupation while sitting in the splendid chair of state provided for him. Sometimes he would study his favorite books and make notes from them, and sometimes he would dictate letters and government orders to a secretary. Thousands of excited Romans around him would be shouting their delight at the sports in the ring, but Aurelius would go on calmly with the work he had in hand.

"I do not like to waste my time by sitting here doing nothing," he would say. "To waste time is one of the greatest of crimes."

And so, by never allowing himself to be idle, Aurelius was able to do many useful things. He established good schools and hospitals in Rome and other cities of Italy. He introduced new trades so that the poor people could get a much better living than before.

Aurelius always gave great encouragement to art and literature. He welcomed authors and artists to Rome and was always their friend. He established libraries and halls of paintings and statuary. He himself wrote several books.

It is said that with all his virtue the life of Aurelius was not a happy one. He had serious troubles at times in governing the Empire, and the cares of a ruler often weighed heavily upon him. His wife, whom he dearly loved, behaved very badly and caused him much anxiety, and his only son was a very bad young man.

So in the latter years of his life Aurelius always appeared melancholy. A smile was seldom seen upon his face. He died at the city now called Vienna, in Austria, 180 A.D.

CONSTANTINE THE GREAT

I

For more than a hundred years after the time of Marcus Aurelius none of the Roman emperors did anything great or remarkable. They were nearly all bad men, and many of them were put to death for their evil deeds.

In the year 307 A.D. the Empire had been divided up through many quarrels and wars between generals of the armies. Often an army would declare its commander an emperor, and he would set himself up as ruler of part of the Empire. So in this way there came at last to be six persons who claimed to be emperors.

None of them was in any way remarkable except the Emperor Con'stan-tine, called Constantine the Great. He was the son of a former emperor named Con-stan'ti-us. When Constantius died the army chose Constantine to be emperor. But he did not go to Rome to be crowned. He remained in Gaul, for he learned that five others had taken the title of emperor in different parts of the Empire.

After a while, however, Constantine got messages from people in Rome begging him to come and relieve them from the cruel government of Max-en'ti-us, who was acting as emperor there. But Constantine was a wise man. He thought it would not be well for him to leave Gaul and enter into a fight with Maxentius, so he paid no attention to the messages.

At last Maxentius openly insulted Constantine and threatened to kill him. Then Constantine was aroused to

142

anger, so he gathered a great army of good soldiers and set out for Rome. He marched over the Alps and in a short time was fighting the army of Maxentius on the plains of Italy.

The first battle took place near Turin. The soldiers of Maxentius were clad in steel armor; but Constantine's men fought them so fiercely that their armor was of little use to them, and they were speedily defeated. There was another battle at Verona, where Constantine was again the victor.

The third battle took place on the banks of the Tiber, near Rome. Maxentius had more soldiers than Constantine, but he was not a good general, so he was easily beaten. He himself was drowned while fleeing across the Tiber.

After the battle Constantine entered Rome amidst the cheers of the people. A little while afterwards he told an interesting story to a Christian bishop named Eu-se'bi-us. He said that while he was marching through northern Italy, on the way to Rome, he was constantly thinking about the Christian religion. It had been spreading in every civilized country for more than two centuries, and Constantine thought that he, too, should become a Christian and no longer worship pagan gods. But he could not make up his mind to do so.

One day while he was in front of his tent, with his officers and troops around him, there appeared in the heavens an enormous cross of fire. A little on one side of the cross were these words in the Greek language, "By this, conquer." The words are sometimes given in the Latin form, *In hoc signo vinces*, the translation of which is, "Through this sign thou shalt conquer."

Constantine was astonished at the wonderful vision, and he gazed at it until it faded away. He could not understand what it meant and was greatly troubled. But that night he dreamed that Christ appeared to him in robes of dazzling white, bearing a cross in His hands, and that He promised him victory over his enemies if he would make the cross his standard.

Constantine now declared himself a Christian and had a standard made in the form of a cross, with a banner attached to it bearing the initial letters of the name of Christ. This banner was called the *Lab'a-rum*, and it was afterwards the standard of the Roman emperors.

When Constantine became a Christian himself he began to take the Christians into his favor. He made some of them high officers of the government; he built Christian churches and destroyed the pagan temples. He also made the Christian religion the religion of the Empire, and he had the sign of a cross painted on the shields and banners of the Roman armies.

Thus, after many, many years of terrible persecution, the Christians were befriended by the Roman emperor, and soon they became very powerful. Thousands of Romans were converted to Christianity, and the churches were crowded with worshipers.

II

Constantine also very much improved the Roman laws and system of government. He put a stop to the dishonest practices of the officers and established just methods of carrying on public affairs. He disbanded the famous Prætorian Guards, which had been an evil power in Rome for centuries. Many other reforms were carried out by Constantine, who seemed anxious to do what was right and what was for the best interests of the people.

Under Constantine's rule, therefore, Rome was happy and prosperous. To show their gratitude to him for his noble deeds the people erected in his honor a grand marble arch in the central square of the city and inscribed on it:

"TO THE FOUNDER OF OUR PEACE."

Four of the six emperors who had at one time ruled the Empire were now dead. But in the east there was one emperor named Li-cin'i-us. Constantine attacked him, scattered his armies, and took away from him the greater part of his territory.

The two emperors then became friends, but after some time they had a quarrel and went to war again. Each had a large army and a fleet of warships. Two great battles were fought, and Constantine won both. Licinius soon afterwards died.

Now for the first time Constantine was sole emperor, and for more than fourteen years he ruled the immense Roman Empire. He built the most magnificent palace Rome had ever seen. He surrounded himself with hundreds of courtiers and lived in great splendor.

After a time he resolved to move the capital of the Empire to a more central place than Rome, and he selected By-zan'ti-um, an ancient city of Thrace, at the entrance to the Black Sea. To this city Constantine sent numbers of workmen to make alterations and improvements, and he changed its name to Constantinople, which means *city of Constantine*. He spent vast sums of money in erecting gorgeous buildings, making aqueducts, constructing streets and public squares, and in doing the many other things proper to be done in the capital of a great Empire. The finest statues and other works of art that could be obtained in Greece, Italy, and the countries of Asia were brought to make Constantinople beautiful.

When everything was ready Constantine with the officers of his government removed to Constantinople. He lived for about seven years afterwards. There no further wars, except a slight conflict with a tribe called the Goths, and the people of the Empire were contented and prosperous.

Constantine died in Constantinople at the age of sixty-three, after a reign of nearly thirty-one years. He was the first Christian emperor of Rome.

END OF THE WESTERN EMPIRE

Most of the Roman emperors after Constantine were either cruel tyrants or very worthless persons, who spent their time in idle pleasure and neglected their duties to the people. A few, however, did some remarkable things and therefore deserve to be mentioned among the Famous Men.

One emperor, whose name was Ju'li-an, is called in history Julian the Apostate, because he gave up the Christian religion and tried to establish the worship of the pagan gods again in Rome. Julian also attempted to rebuild the Temple of Jerusalem which, as we have seen, was destroyed by Titus. There was a Christian prophecy that it would never be restored, and Julian thought of rebuilding it to prove the prophecy false. A story is told that as soon as the men began the work balls of fire burst from the ground close by them and they had to stop. They tried again and again and the same thing happened, and at last they had to give up the work altogether.

Not long after he became emperor Julian set out with a large army to conquer Persia. For a while he was very successful and defeated the Persian king in many battles. But one day he was shot in the breast by an arrow and he died soon after. It is said that while he lay wounded he cast a handful of his own blood toward heaven, crying out, "Thou hast conquered, O Galilean." By Galilean he meant Christ, who is sometimes called the Galilean because He was brought up in Galilee.

Not long after the reign of Julian, there was an emperor named Val-en-tin'i-an. He made his brother Va'lens emperor of the eastern part of the Empire while he himself ruled over the western part. And for many years afterwards the Empire was ruled in this way by two emperors, one called the Emperor of the East, and the other the Emperor of the West.

On the death of Valentinian his son Gra'ti-an became Emperor of the West, and a talented soldier named The-o-do'si-us became Emperor of the East on the death of Valens. Gratian was weak and unfit to rule, and he was killed by a Spaniard named Max'i-mus, who made himself Emperor of the West.

Theodosius fought Maximus and defeated him, and afterwards had him put to death. Then he made a son of Valentinian Emperor of the West, as Valentinian II, and gave him as his adviser a chief named Ar-bo-gas'tes. But Arbogastes was soon the real master of the Western Empire. One day Valentinian was found dead in his bed, and Arbogastes then made Eu-ge'ni-us, a teacher, the emperor. Theodosius, who well knew that Valentinian II had been murdered, made war on Eugenius and Arbogastes and defeated them, and until his death, a few months afterwards (in 395), Theodosius was emperor of both East and West.

Theodosius had been a wise ruler, but he did one very bad thing. The people of Thes-sa-lo-ni'ca, a city of Macedonia, a country north of Greece, had killed their governor because he had put one of their favorite circus riders in prison. When Theodosius heard of this he was very angry, and he gave orders that they should be invited to a show in the circus and there put to death. This cruel order was carried out. The citizens of Thessalonica were invited to come one day to the circus to see a grand show. Thousands came, and as soon as they had taken their seats a troop of soldiers under the command of one of the generals of Theodosius entered the building and massacred them all without mercy.

Over six thousand men, women, and children were killed.

At this time Theodosius resided in Milan, a city of north Italy. At the same time there lived in Milan a bishop named Am'brose, who was a good and holy man. When Ambrose was told of the massacre at Thessalonica he was greatly shocked. He severely reprimanded the emperor and would not permit him to enter the door of the church until he had done penance for the sin he had committed in so cruelly putting to death many innocent persons.

The successor of Theodosius as Emperor of the West was his son Hon-o'ri-us, who reigned for twenty-nine years; but the actual ruler during all that time was a soldier named Stil'i-cho, who was the emperor's guardian. Honorius was a simpleton and had no desire or ability to attend to the affairs of the government.

The Goths and Vandals and other barbarous tribes from the north and east of Europe now began to overrun the Western Empire and to threaten Rome itself. Twice the great city was actually captured and plundered; the first time by the Goths under Al'ar-ic, and next by the Vandals under a bold warrior named Gen'ser-ic. About those barbarian chiefs and their exploits you will perhaps read in FAMOUS MEN OF THE MIDDLE AGES, a companion volume to this book.

To defend the seat of their Empire against the attacks of its enemies the Romans were obliged to withdraw their forces from several of the outlying provinces, including Britain, which was now left to its native inhabitants. For more than fifty years afterwards a number of men without much ability took part in ruling what was left of the once mighty Empire. One of these was called by the high-sounding name of Romulus Augustulus. He was the son of O-res'tes, the general of the army of Italy and had been made emperor by his father. He was the last of the Western emperors.

Among the Italian soldiers there was a huge, half-savage man named O-do-a'cer, who belonged to a wild northern tribe. He was a favorite of the army because of his courage and strength. He resolved to be the ruler of Italy, so with the army at his back he put Orestes to death, took Romulus Augustulus prisoner, and forced him to give up the title of emperor. Then Odoacer became king of Italy in the year 476 A.D.

By this time the world had nearly entered that period which is known as the Middle Ages, and many of the other countries which had been parts of the Roman Empire were either ruling themselves or defending themselves against new invaders. Gaul was invaded and conquered by German tribes called Franks, from whom the country subsequently got the name of France. Britain, abandoned by the Romans, was soon after conquered by other German tribes. And so at last the great Roman Empire had crumbled to pieces, and Rome, so long the Mistress of the World, as she was called, had fallen from her proud position of grandeur and power into that of a second or third rate city.

But the Empire of the East continued to exist for centuries afterwards, with Constantinople as its capital. It included many of the countries of Asia, Africa, and eastern Europe which had formerly belonged to the undivided Empire. In course of time the power of the Greeks, aided by the influence of the Greek division of the Church, became supreme at Constantinople, and so the Empire was also called the Greek Empire, and sometimes the Byzantine Empire, from the ancient name of the capital.

In the fourteenth century the Turks, or Mohammedans, then very powerful in southwestern Asia, began to make inroads on the Empire. They conquered and took possession of several of its provinces, and in 1453 they captured Constantinople, which has since been the capital of the Turkish, or Ottoman Empire, the ruler of which is known as the sultan.

THE END

A CATALOG OF SELECTED
DOVER BOOKS
IN ALL FIELDS OF INTEREST

A CATALOG OF SELECTED DOVER
BOOKS IN ALL FIELDS OF INTEREST

CONCERNING THE SPIRITUAL IN ART, Wassily Kandinsky. Pioneering work by father of abstract art. Thoughts on color theory, nature of art. Analysis of earlier masters. 12 illustrations. 80pp. of text. 5⅜ x 8½. 0-486-23411-8

CELTIC ART: The Methods of Construction, George Bain. Simple geometric techniques for making Celtic interlacements, spirals, Kells-type initials, animals, humans, etc. Over 500 illustrations. 160pp. 9 x 12. (Available in U.S. only.) 0-486-22923-8

AN ATLAS OF ANATOMY FOR ARTISTS, Fritz Schider. Most thorough reference work on art anatomy in the world. Hundreds of illustrations, including selections from works by Vesalius, Leonardo, Goya, Ingres, Michelangelo, others. 593 illustrations. 192pp. 7⅛ x 10¼. 0-486-20241-0

CELTIC HAND STROKE-BY-STROKE (Irish Half-Uncial from "The Book of Kells"): An Arthur Baker Calligraphy Manual, Arthur Baker. Complete guide to creating each letter of the alphabet in distinctive Celtic manner. Covers hand position, strokes, pens, inks, paper, more. Illustrated. 48pp. 8¼ x 11. 0-486-24336-2

EASY ORIGAMI, John Montroll. Charming collection of 32 projects (hat, cup, pelican, piano, swan, many more) specially designed for the novice origami hobbyist. Clearly illustrated easy-to-follow instructions insure that even beginning papercrafters will achieve successful results. 48pp. 8¼ x 11. 0-486-27298-2

BLOOMINGDALE'S ILLUSTRATED 1886 CATALOG: Fashions, Dry Goods and Housewares, Bloomingdale Brothers. Famed merchants' extremely rare catalog depicting about 1,700 products: clothing, housewares, firearms, dry goods, jewelry, more. Invaluable for dating, identifying vintage items. Also, copyright-free graphics for artists, designers. Co-published with Henry Ford Museum & Greenfield Village. 160pp. 8¼ x 11. 0-486-25780-0

THE ART OF WORLDLY WISDOM, Baltasar Gracian. "Think with the few and speak with the many," "Friends are a second existence," and "Be able to forget" are among this 1637 volume's 300 pithy maxims. A perfect source of mental and spiritual refreshment, it can be opened at random and appreciated either in brief or at length. 128pp. 5⅜ x 8½. 0-486-44034-6

JOHNSON'S DICTIONARY: A Modern Selection, Samuel Johnson (E. L. McAdam and George Milne, eds.). This modern version reduces the original 1755 edition's 2,300 pages of definitions and literary examples to a more manageable length, retaining the verbal pleasure and historical curiosity of the original. 480pp. 5³⁄₁₆ x 8¼. 0-486-44089-3

ADVENTURES OF HUCKLEBERRY FINN, Mark Twain, Illustrated by E. W. Kemble. A work of eternal richness and complexity, a source of ongoing critical debate, and a literary landmark, Twain's 1885 masterpiece about a barefoot boy's journey of self-discovery has enthralled readers around the world. This handsome clothbound reproduction of the first edition features all 174 of the original black-and-white illustrations. 368pp. 5⅜ x 8½. 0-486-44322-1

STICKLEY CRAFTSMAN FURNITURE CATALOGS, Gustav Stickley and L. & J. G. Stickley. Beautiful, functional furniture in two authentic catalogs from 1910. 594 illustrations, including 277 photos, show settles, rockers, armchairs, reclining chairs, bookcases, desks, tables. 183pp. 6½ x 9¼.   0-486-23838-5

AMERICAN LOCOMOTIVES IN HISTORIC PHOTOGRAPHS: 1858 to 1949, Ron Ziel (ed.). A rare collection of 126 meticulously detailed official photographs, called "builder portraits," of American locomotives that majestically chronicle the rise of steam locomotive power in America. Introduction. Detailed captions. xi+ 129pp. 9 x 12.   0-486-27393-8

AMERICA'S LIGHTHOUSES: An Illustrated History, Francis Ross Holland, Jr. Delightfully written, profusely illustrated fact-filled survey of over 200 American light-houses since 1716. History, anecdotes, technological advances, more. 240pp. 8 x 10¾.
                    0-486-25576-X

TOWARDS A NEW ARCHITECTURE, Le Corbusier. Pioneering manifesto by founder of "International School." Technical and aesthetic theories, views of industry, eco-nomics, relation of form to function, "mass-production split" and much more. Profusely illustrated. 320pp. 6⅛ x 9¼. (Available in U.S. only.)   0-486-25023-7

HOW THE OTHER HALF LIVES, Jacob Riis. Famous journalistic record, expos-ing poverty and degradation of New York slums around 1900, by major social reformer. 100 striking and influential photographs. 233pp. 10 x 7⅞.   0-486-22012-5

FRUIT KEY AND TWIG KEY TO TREES AND SHRUBS, William M. Harlow. One of the handiest and most widely used identification aids. Fruit key covers 120 deciduous and evergreen species; twig key 160 deciduous species. Easily used. Over 300 photographs. 126pp. 5⅜ x 8½.   0-486-20511-8

COMMON BIRD SONGS, Dr. Donald J. Borror. Songs of 60 most common U.S. birds: robins, sparrows, cardinals, bluejays, finches, more—arranged in order of increasing complexity. Up to 9 variations of songs of each species.
                    Cassette and manual 0-486-99911-4

ORCHIDS AS HOUSE PLANTS, Rebecca Tyson Northen. Grow cattleyas and many other kinds of orchids—in a window, in a case, or under artificial light. 63 illus-trations. 148pp. 5⅜ x 8½.   0-486-23261-1

MONSTER MAZES, Dave Phillips. Masterful mazes at four levels of difficulty. Avoid deadly perils and evil creatures to find magical treasures. Solutions for all 32 exciting illustrated puzzles. 48pp. 8¼ x 11.   0-486-26005-4

MOZART'S DON GIOVANNI (DOVER OPERA LIBRETTO SERIES), Wolfgang Amadeus Mozart. Introduced and translated by Ellen H. Bleiler. Standard Italian libretto, with complete English translation. Convenient and thoroughly portable—an ideal companion for reading along with a recording or the performance itself. Introduction. List of characters. Plot summary. 121pp. 5¼ x 8½. 0-486-24944-1

FRANK LLOYD WRIGHT'S DANA HOUSE, Donald Hoffmann. Pictorial essay of residential masterpiece with over 160 interior and exterior photos, plans, eleva-tions, sketches and studies. 128pp. 9¼ x 10¾.   0-486-29120-0

THE CLARINET AND CLARINET PLAYING, David Pino. Lively, comprehensive work features suggestions about technique, musicianship, and musical interpretation, as well as guidelines for teaching, making your own reeds, and preparing for public performance. Includes an intriguing look at clarinet history. "A godsend," *The Clarinet,* Journal of the International Clarinet Society. Appendixes. 7 illus. 320pp. 5⅜ x 8½. 0-486-40270-3

HOLLYWOOD GLAMOR PORTRAITS, John Kobal (ed.). 145 photos from 1926-49. Harlow, Gable, Bogart, Bacall; 94 stars in all. Full background on photographers, technical aspects. 160pp. 8⅜ x 11¼. 0-486-23352-9

THE RAVEN AND OTHER FAVORITE POEMS, Edgar Allan Poe. Over 40 of the author's most memorable poems: "The Bells," "Ulalume," "Israfel," "To Helen," "The Conqueror Worm," "Eldorado," "Annabel Lee," many more. Alphabetic lists of titles and first lines. 64pp. 5³⁄₁₆ x 8¼. 0-486-26685-0

PERSONAL MEMOIRS OF U. S. GRANT, Ulysses Simpson Grant. Intelligent, deeply moving firsthand account of Civil War campaigns, considered by many the finest military memoirs ever written. Includes letters, historic photographs, maps and more. 528pp. 6⅛ x 9¼. 0-486-28587-1

ANCIENT EGYPTIAN MATERIALS AND INDUSTRIES, A. Lucas and J. Harris. Fascinating, comprehensive, thoroughly documented text describes this ancient civilization's vast resources and the processes that incorporated them in daily life, including the use of animal products, building materials, cosmetics, perfumes and incense, fibers, glazed ware, glass and its manufacture, materials used in the mummification process, and much more. 544pp. 6⅛ x 9¼. (Available in U.S. only.) 0-486-40446-3

RUSSIAN STORIES/RUSSKIE RASSKAZY: A Dual-Language Book, edited by Gleb Struve. Twelve tales by such masters as Chekhov, Tolstoy, Dostoevsky, Pushkin, others. Excellent word-for-word English translations on facing pages, plus teaching and study aids, Russian/English vocabulary, biographical/critical introductions, more. 416pp. 5⅜ x 8½. 0-486-26244-8

PHILADELPHIA THEN AND NOW: 60 Sites Photographed in the Past and Present, Kenneth Finkel and Susan Oyama. Rare photographs of City Hall, Logan Square, Independence Hall, Betsy Ross House, other landmarks juxtaposed with contemporary views. Captures changing face of historic city. Introduction. Captions. 128pp. 8¼ x 11. 0-486-25790-8

NORTH AMERICAN INDIAN LIFE: Customs and Traditions of 23 Tribes, Elsie Clews Parsons (ed.). 27 fictionalized essays by noted anthropologists examine religion, customs, government, additional facets of life among the Winnebago, Crow, Zuni, Eskimo, other tribes. 480pp. 6⅛ x 9¼. 0-486-27377-6

TECHNICAL MANUAL AND DICTIONARY OF CLASSICAL BALLET, Gail Grant. Defines, explains, comments on steps, movements, poses and concepts. 15-page pictorial section. Basic book for student, viewer. 127pp. 5⅜ x 8½. 0-486-21843-0

THE MALE AND FEMALE FIGURE IN MOTION: 60 Classic Photographic Sequences, Eadweard Muybridge. 60 true-action photographs of men and women walking, running, climbing, bending, turning, etc., reproduced from rare 19th-century masterpiece. vi + 121pp. 9 x 12. 0-486-24745-7

ANIMALS: 1,419 Copyright-Free Illustrations of Mammals, Birds, Fish, Insects, etc., Jim Harter (ed.). Clear wood engravings present, in extremely lifelike poses, over 1,000 species of animals. One of the most extensive pictorial sourcebooks of its kind. Captions. Index. 284pp. 9 x 12. 0-486-23766-4

1001 QUESTIONS ANSWERED ABOUT THE SEASHORE, N. J. Berrill and Jacquelyn Berrill. Queries answered about dolphins, sea snails, sponges, starfish, fishes, shore birds, many others. Covers appearance, breeding, growth, feeding, much more. 305pp. 5¼ x 8¼. 0-486-23366-9

ATTRACTING BIRDS TO YOUR YARD, William J. Weber. Easy-to-follow guide offers advice on how to attract the greatest diversity of birds: birdhouses, feeders, water and waterers, much more. 96pp. 5³⁄₁₆ x 8¼. 0-486-28927-3

MEDICINAL AND OTHER USES OF NORTH AMERICAN PLANTS: A Historical Survey with Special Reference to the Eastern Indian Tribes, Charlotte Erichsen-Brown. Chronological historical citations document 500 years of usage of plants, trees, shrubs native to eastern Canada, northeastern U.S. Also complete identifying information. 343 illustrations. 544pp. 6½ x 9¼. 0-486-25951-X

STORYBOOK MAZES, Dave Phillips. 23 stories and mazes on two-page spreads: Wizard of Oz, Treasure Island, Robin Hood, etc. Solutions. 64pp. 8¼ x 11. 0-486-23628-5

AMERICAN NEGRO SONGS: 230 Folk Songs and Spirituals, Religious and Secular, John W. Work. This authoritative study traces the African influences of songs sung and played by black Americans at work, in church, and as entertainment. The author discusses the lyric significance of such songs as "Swing Low, Sweet Chariot," "John Henry," and others and offers the words and music for 230 songs. Bibliography. Index of Song Titles. 272pp. 6½ x 9¼. 0-486-40271-1

MOVIE-STAR PORTRAITS OF THE FORTIES, John Kobal (ed.). 163 glamor, studio photos of 106 stars of the 1940s: Rita Hayworth, Ava Gardner, Marlon Brando, Clark Gable, many more. 176pp. 8⅜ x 11¼. 0-486-23546-7

YEKL and THE IMPORTED BRIDEGROOM AND OTHER STORIES OF YIDDISH NEW YORK, Abraham Cahan. Film Hester Street based on Yekl (1896). Novel, other stories among first about Jewish immigrants on N.Y.'s East Side. 240pp. 5⅜ x 8½. 0-486-22427-9

SELECTED POEMS, Walt Whitman. Generous sampling from Leaves of Grass. Twenty-four poems include "I Hear America Singing," "Song of the Open Road," "I Sing the Body Electric," "When Lilacs Last in the Dooryard Bloom'd," "O Captain! My Captain!"–all reprinted from an authoritative edition. Lists of titles and first lines. 128pp. 5³⁄₁₆ x 8¼. 0-486-26878-0

SONGS OF EXPERIENCE: Facsimile Reproduction with 26 Plates in Full Color, William Blake. 26 full-color plates from a rare 1826 edition. Includes "The Tyger," "London," "Holy Thursday," and other poems. Printed text of poems. 48pp. 5¼ x 7. 0-486-24636-1

THE BEST TALES OF HOFFMANN, E. T. A. Hoffmann. 10 of Hoffmann's most important stories: "Nutcracker and the King of Mice," "The Golden Flowerpot," etc. 458pp. 5⅜ x 8½. 0-486-21793-0

THE BOOK OF TEA, Kakuzo Okakura. Minor classic of the Orient: entertaining, charming explanation, interpretation of traditional Japanese culture in terms of tea ceremony. 94pp. 5⅜ x 8½. 0-486-20070-1

FRENCH STORIES/CONTES FRANÇAIS: A Dual-Language Book, Wallace Fowlie. Ten stories by French masters, Voltaire to Camus: "Micromegas" by Voltaire; "The Atheist's Mass" by Balzac; "Minuet" by de Maupassant; "The Guest" by Camus, six more. Excellent English translations on facing pages. Also French-English vocabulary list, exercises, more. 352pp. 5⅜ x 8½.   0-486-26443-2

CHICAGO AT THE TURN OF THE CENTURY IN PHOTOGRAPHS: 122 Historic Views from the Collections of the Chicago Historical Society, Larry A. Viskochil. Rare large-format prints offer detailed views of City Hall, State Street, the Loop, Hull House, Union Station, many other landmarks, circa 1904-1913. Introduction. Captions. Maps. 144pp. 9⅜ x 12¼.   0-486-24656-6

OLD BROOKLYN IN EARLY PHOTOGRAPHS, 1865-1929, William Lee Younger. Luna Park, Gravesend race track, construction of Grand Army Plaza, moving of Hotel Brighton, etc. 157 previously unpublished photographs. 165pp. 8⅞ x 11¾.   0-486-23587-4

THE MYTHS OF THE NORTH AMERICAN INDIANS, Lewis Spence. Rich anthology of the myths and legends of the Algonquins, Iroquois, Pawnees and Sioux, prefaced by an extensive historical and ethnological commentary. 36 illustrations. 480pp. 5⅜ x 8½.   0-486-25967-6

AN ENCYCLOPEDIA OF BATTLES: Accounts of Over 1,560 Battles from 1479 B.C. to the Present, David Eggenberger. Essential details of every major battle in recorded history from the first battle of Megiddo in 1479 B.C. to Grenada in 1984. List of Battle Maps. New Appendix covering the years 1967-1984. Index. 99 illustrations. 544pp. 6½ x 9¼.   0-486-24913-1

SAILING ALONE AROUND THE WORLD, Captain Joshua Slocum. First man to sail around the world, alone, in small boat. One of great feats of seamanship told in delightful manner. 67 illustrations. 294pp. 5⅜ x 8½.   0-486-20326-3

ANARCHISM AND OTHER ESSAYS, Emma Goldman. Powerful, penetrating, prophetic essays on direct action, role of minorities, prison reform, puritan hypocrisy, violence, etc. 271pp. 5⅜ x 8½.   0-486-22484-8

MYTHS OF THE HINDUS AND BUDDHISTS, Ananda K. Coomaraswamy and Sister Nivedita. Great stories of the epics; deeds of Krishna, Shiva, taken from puranas, Vedas, folk tales; etc. 32 illustrations. 400pp. 5⅜ x 8½.   0-486-21759-0

MY BONDAGE AND MY FREEDOM, Frederick Douglass. Born a slave, Douglass became outspoken force in antislavery movement. The best of Douglass' autobiographies. Graphic description of slave life. 464pp. 5⅜ x 8½.   0-486-22457-0

FOLLOWING THE EQUATOR: A Journey Around the World, Mark Twain. Fascinating humorous account of 1897 voyage to Hawaii, Australia, India, New Zealand, etc. Ironic, bemused reports on peoples, customs, climate, flora and fauna, politics, much more. 197 illustrations. 720pp. 5⅜ x 8½.   0-486-26113-1

THE PEOPLE CALLED SHAKERS, Edward D. Andrews. Definitive study of Shakers: origins, beliefs, practices, dances, social organization, furniture and crafts, etc. 33 illustrations. 351pp. 5⅜ x 8½.   0-486-21081-2

THE MYTHS OF GREECE AND ROME, H. A. Guerber. A classic of mythology, generously illustrated, long prized for its simple, graphic, accurate retelling of the principal myths of Greece and Rome, and for its commentary on their origins and significance. With 64 illustrations by Michelangelo, Raphael, Titian, Rubens, Canova, Bernini and others. 480pp. 5⅜ x 8½.   0-486-27584-1

PSYCHOLOGY OF MUSIC, Carl E. Seashore. Classic work discusses music as a medium from psychological viewpoint. Clear treatment of physical acoustics, auditory apparatus, sound perception, development of musical skills, nature of musical feeling, host of other topics. 88 figures. 408pp. 5⅜ x 8½.   0-486-21851-1

LIFE IN ANCIENT EGYPT, Adolf Erman. Fullest, most thorough, detailed older account with much not in more recent books, domestic life, religion, magic, medicine, commerce, much more. Many illustrations reproduce tomb paintings, carvings, hieroglyphs, etc. 597pp. 5⅜ x 8½.   0-486-22632-8

SUNDIALS, Their Theory and Construction, Albert Waugh. Far and away the best, most thorough coverage of ideas, mathematics concerned, types, construction, adjusting anywhere. Simple, nontechnical treatment allows even children to build several of these dials. Over 100 illustrations. 230pp. 5⅜ x 8½.   0-486-22947-5

THEORETICAL HYDRODYNAMICS, L. M. Milne-Thomson. Classic exposition of the mathematical theory of fluid motion, applicable to both hydrodynamics and aerodynamics. Over 600 exercises. 768pp. 6⅛ x 9¼.   0-486-68970-0

OLD-TIME VIGNETTES IN FULL COLOR, Carol Belanger Grafton (ed.). Over 390 charming, often sentimental illustrations, selected from archives of Victorian graphics—pretty women posing, children playing, food, flowers, kittens and puppies, smiling cherubs, birds and butterflies, much more. All copyright-free. 48pp. 9¼ x 12¼.
0-486-27269-9

PERSPECTIVE FOR ARTISTS, Rex Vicat Cole. Depth, perspective of sky and sea, shadows, much more, not usually covered. 391 diagrams, 81 reproductions of drawings and paintings. 279pp. 5⅜ x 8½.   0-486-22487-2

DRAWING THE LIVING FIGURE, Joseph Sheppard. Innovative approach to artistic anatomy focuses on specifics of surface anatomy, rather than muscles and bones. Over 170 drawings of live models in front, back and side views, and in widely varying poses. Accompanying diagrams. 177 illustrations. Introduction. Index. 144pp. 8⅜ x11¼.   0-486-26723-7

GOTHIC AND OLD ENGLISH ALPHABETS: 100 Complete Fonts, Dan X. Solo. Add power, elegance to posters, signs, other graphics with 100 stunning copyright-free alphabets: Blackstone, Dolbey, Germania, 97 more—including many lower-case, numerals, punctuation marks. 104pp. 8⅛ x 11.   0-486-24695-7

THE BOOK OF WOOD CARVING, Charles Marshall Sayers. Finest book for beginners discusses fundamentals and offers 34 designs. "Absolutely first rate . . . well thought out and well executed."—E. J. Tangerman. 118pp. 7¾ x 10⅝.   0-486-23654-4

ILLUSTRATED CATALOG OF CIVIL WAR MILITARY GOODS: Union Army Weapons, Insignia, Uniform Accessories, and Other Equipment, Schuyler, Hartley, and Graham. Rare, profusely illustrated 1846 catalog includes Union Army uniform and dress regulations, arms and ammunition, coats, insignia, flags, swords, rifles, etc. 226 illustrations. 160pp. 9 x 12.   0-486-24939-5

WOMEN'S FASHIONS OF THE EARLY 1900s: An Unabridged Republication of "New York Fashions, 1909," National Cloak & Suit Co. Rare catalog of mail-order fashions documents women's and children's clothing styles shortly after the turn of the century. Captions offer full descriptions, prices. Invaluable resource for fashion, costume historians. Approximately 725 illustrations. 128pp. 8⅜ x 11¼.
0-486-27276-1

HOW TO DO BEADWORK, Mary White. Fundamental book on craft from simple projects to five-bead chains and woven works. 106 illustrations. 142pp. $5\frac{3}{8}$ x 8. 0-486-20697-1

THE 1912 AND 1915 GUSTAV STICKLEY FURNITURE CATALOGS, Gustav Stickley. With over 200 detailed illustrations and descriptions, these two catalogs are essential reading and reference materials and identification guides for Stickley furniture. Captions cite materials, dimensions and prices. 112pp. $6\frac{1}{2}$ x $9\frac{1}{4}$. 0-486-26676-1

EARLY AMERICAN LOCOMOTIVES, John H. White, Jr. Finest locomotive engravings from early 19th century: historical (1804–74), main-line (after 1870), special, foreign, etc. 147 plates. 142pp. $11\frac{3}{8}$ x $8\frac{1}{4}$. 0-486-22772-3

LITTLE BOOK OF EARLY AMERICAN CRAFTS AND TRADES, Peter Stockham (ed.). 1807 children's book explains crafts and trades: baker, hatter, cooper, potter, and many others. 23 copperplate illustrations. 140pp. $4\frac{5}{8}$ x 6. 0-486-23336-7

VICTORIAN FASHIONS AND COSTUMES FROM HARPER'S BAZAR, 1867–1898, Stella Blum (ed.). Day costumes, evening wear, sports clothes, shoes, hats, other accessories in over 1,000 detailed engravings. 320pp. $9\frac{3}{8}$ x $12\frac{1}{4}$. 0-486-22990-4

THE LONG ISLAND RAIL ROAD IN EARLY PHOTOGRAPHS, Ron Ziel. Over 220 rare photos, informative text document origin (1844) and development of rail service on Long Island. Vintage views of early trains, locomotives, stations, passengers, crews, much more. Captions. $8\frac{7}{8}$ x $11\frac{3}{4}$. 0-486-26301-0

VOYAGE OF THE LIBERDADE, Joshua Slocum. Great 19th-century mariner's thrilling, first-hand account of the wreck of his ship off South America, the 35-foot boat he built from the wreckage, and its remarkable voyage home. 128pp. $5\frac{3}{8}$ x $8\frac{1}{2}$. 0-486-40022-0

TEN BOOKS ON ARCHITECTURE, Vitruvius. The most important book ever written on architecture. Early Roman aesthetics, technology, classical orders, site selection, all other aspects. Morgan translation. 331pp. $5\frac{3}{8}$ x $8\frac{1}{2}$. 0-486-20645-9

THE HUMAN FIGURE IN MOTION, Eadweard Muybridge. More than 4,500 stopped-action photos, in action series, showing undraped men, women, children jumping, lying down, throwing, sitting, wrestling, carrying, etc. 390pp. $7\frac{7}{8}$ x $10\frac{5}{8}$. 0-486-20204-6 Clothbd.

TREES OF THE EASTERN AND CENTRAL UNITED STATES AND CANADA, William M. Harlow. Best one-volume guide to 140 trees. Full descriptions, woodlore, range, etc. Over 600 illustrations. Handy size. 288pp. $4\frac{1}{2}$ x $6\frac{3}{8}$. 0-486-20395-6

GROWING AND USING HERBS AND SPICES, Milo Miloradovich. Versatile handbook provides all the information needed for cultivation and use of all the herbs and spices available in North America. 4 illustrations. Index. Glossary. 236pp. $5\frac{3}{8}$ x $8\frac{1}{2}$. 0-486-25058-X

BIG BOOK OF MAZES AND LABYRINTHS, Walter Shepherd. 50 mazes and labyrinths in all–classical, solid, ripple, and more–in one great volume. Perfect inexpensive puzzler for clever youngsters. Full solutions. 112pp. $8\frac{1}{8}$ x 11. 0-486-22951-3

PIANO TUNING, J. Cree Fischer. Clearest, best book for beginner, amateur. Simple repairs, raising dropped notes, tuning by easy method of flattened fifths. No previous skills needed. 4 illustrations. 201pp. $5\frac{3}{8}$ x $8\frac{1}{2}$. 0-486-23267-0

HINTS TO SINGERS, Lillian Nordica. Selecting the right teacher, developing confidence, overcoming stage fright, and many other important skills receive thoughtful discussion in this indispensible guide, written by a world-famous diva of four decades' experience. 96pp. $5\frac{3}{8}$ x $8\frac{1}{2}$. 0-486-40094-8

THE COMPLETE NONSENSE OF EDWARD LEAR, Edward Lear. All nonsense limericks, zany alphabets, Owl and Pussycat, songs, nonsense botany, etc., illustrated by Lear. Total of 320pp. $5\frac{3}{8}$ x $8\frac{1}{2}$. (Available in U.S. only.) 0-486-20167-8

VICTORIAN PARLOUR POETRY: An Annotated Anthology, Michael R. Turner. 117 gems by Longfellow, Tennyson, Browning, many lesser-known poets. "The Village Blacksmith," "Curfew Must Not Ring Tonight," "Only a Baby Small," dozens more, often difficult to find elsewhere. Index of poets, titles, first lines. xxiii + 325pp. $5\frac{5}{8}$ x $8\frac{1}{4}$. 0-486-27044-0

DUBLINERS, James Joyce. Fifteen stories offer vivid, tightly focused observations of the lives of Dublin's poorer classes. At least one, "The Dead," is considered a masterpiece. Reprinted complete and unabridged from standard edition. 160pp. $5\frac{3}{16}$ x $8\frac{1}{4}$. 0-486-26870-5

GREAT WEIRD TALES: 14 Stories by Lovecraft, Blackwood, Machen and Others, S. T. Joshi (ed.). 14 spellbinding tales, including "The Sin Eater," by Fiona McLeod, "The Eye Above the Mantel," by Frank Belknap Long, as well as renowned works by R. H. Barlow, Lord Dunsany, Arthur Machen, W. C. Morrow and eight other masters of the genre. 256pp. $5\frac{3}{8}$ x $8\frac{1}{2}$. (Available in U.S. only.) 0-486-40436-6

THE BOOK OF THE SACRED MAGIC OF ABRAMELIN THE MAGE, translated by S. MacGregor Mathers. Medieval manuscript of ceremonial magic. Basic document in Aleister Crowley, Golden Dawn groups. 268pp. $5\frac{3}{8}$ x $8\frac{1}{2}$. 0-486-23211-5

THE BATTLES THAT CHANGED HISTORY, Fletcher Pratt. Eminent historian profiles 16 crucial conflicts, ancient to modern, that changed the course of civilization. 352pp. $5\frac{3}{8}$ x $8\frac{1}{2}$. 0-486-41129-X

NEW RUSSIAN-ENGLISH AND ENGLISH-RUSSIAN DICTIONARY, M. A. O'Brien. This is a remarkably handy Russian dictionary, containing a surprising amount of information, including over 70,000 entries. 366pp. $4\frac{1}{2}$ x $6\frac{1}{8}$. 0-486-20208-9

NEW YORK IN THE FORTIES, Andreas Feininger. 162 brilliant photographs by the well-known photographer, formerly with *Life* magazine. Commuters, shoppers, Times Square at night, much else from city at its peak. Captions by John von Hartz. 181pp. $9\frac{1}{4}$ x $10\frac{3}{4}$. 0-486-23585-8

INDIAN SIGN LANGUAGE, William Tomkins. Over 525 signs developed by Sioux and other tribes. Written instructions and diagrams. Also 290 pictographs. 111pp. $6\frac{1}{8}$ x $9\frac{1}{4}$. 0-486-22029-X

ANATOMY: A Complete Guide for Artists, Joseph Sheppard. A master of figure drawing shows artists how to render human anatomy convincingly. Over 460 illustrations. 224pp. $8\frac{3}{8}$ x $11\frac{1}{4}$. 0-486-27279-6

MEDIEVAL CALLIGRAPHY: Its History and Technique, Marc Drogin. Spirited history, comprehensive instruction manual covers 13 styles (ca. 4th century through 15th). Excellent photographs; directions for duplicating medieval techniques with modern tools. 224pp. $8\frac{3}{8}$ x $11\frac{1}{4}$. 0-486-26142-5

DRIED FLOWERS: How to Prepare Them, Sarah Whitlock and Martha Rankin. Complete instructions on how to use silica gel, meal and borax, perlite aggregate, sand and borax, glycerine and water to create attractive permanent flower arrangements. 12 illustrations. 32pp. 5⅜ x 8½. 0-486-21802-3

EASY-TO-MAKE BIRD FEEDERS FOR WOODWORKERS, Scott D. Campbell. Detailed, simple-to-use guide for designing, constructing, caring for and using feeders. Text, illustrations for 12 classic and contemporary designs. 96pp. 5⅜ x 8½. 0-486-25847-5

THE COMPLETE BOOK OF BIRDHOUSE CONSTRUCTION FOR WOOD-WORKERS, Scott D. Campbell. Detailed instructions, illustrations, tables. Also data on bird habitat and instinct patterns. Bibliography. 3 tables. 63 illustrations in 15 figures. 48pp. 5¼ x 8½. 0-486-24407-5

SCOTTISH WONDER TALES FROM MYTH AND LEGEND, Donald A. Mackenzie. 16 lively tales tell of giants rumbling down mountainsides, of a magic wand that turns stone pillars into warriors, of gods and goddesses, evil hags, powerful forces and more. 240pp. 5⅜ x 8½. 0-486-29677-6

THE HISTORY OF UNDERCLOTHES, C. Willett Cunnington and Phyllis Cunnington. Fascinating, well-documented survey covering six centuries of English undergarments, enhanced with over 100 illustrations: 12th-century laced-up bodice, footed long drawers (1795), 19th-century bustles, l9th-century corsets for men, Victorian "bust improvers," much more. 272pp. 5⅜ x 8¼. 0-486-27124-2

ARTS AND CRAFTS FURNITURE: The Complete Brooks Catalog of 1912, Brooks Manufacturing Co. Photos and detailed descriptions of more than 150 now very collectible furniture designs from the Arts and Crafts movement depict davenports, settees, buffets, desks, tables, chairs, bedsteads, dressers and more, all built of solid, quarter-sawed oak. Invaluable for students and enthusiasts of antiques, Americana and the decorative arts. 80pp. 6½ x 9¼. 0-486-27471-3

WILBUR AND ORVILLE: A Biography of the Wright Brothers, Fred Howard. Definitive, crisply written study tells the full story of the brothers' lives and work. A vividly written biography, unparalleled in scope and color, that also captures the spirit of an extraordinary era. 560pp. 6⅛ x 9¼. 0-486-40297-5

THE ARTS OF THE SAILOR: Knotting, Splicing and Ropework, Hervey Garrett Smith. Indispensable shipboard reference covers tools, basic knots and useful hitches; handsewing and canvas work, more. Over 100 illustrations. Delightful reading for sea lovers. 256pp. 5⅜ x 8½. 0-486-26440-8

FRANK LLOYD WRIGHT'S FALLINGWATER: The House and Its History, Second, Revised Edition, Donald Hoffmann. A total revision–both in text and illustrations–of the standard document on Fallingwater, the boldest, most personal architectural statement of Wright's mature years, updated with valuable new material from the recently opened Frank Lloyd Wright Archives. "Fascinating"–The New York Times. 116 illustrations. 128pp. 9¼ x 10¾. 0-486-27430-6

PHOTOGRAPHIC SKETCHBOOK OF THE CIVIL WAR, Alexander Gardner. 100 photos taken on field during the Civil War. Famous shots of Manassas Harper's Ferry, Lincoln, Richmond, slave pens, etc. 244pp. 10⅝ x 8¼. 0-486-22731-6

FIVE ACRES AND INDEPENDENCE, Maurice G. Kains. Great back-to-the-land classic explains basics of self-sufficient farming. The one book to get. 95 illustrations. 397pp. 5⅜ x 8½. 0-486-20974-1

A MODERN HERBAL, Margaret Grieve. Much the fullest, most exact, most useful compilation of herbal material. Gigantic alphabetical encyclopedia, from aconite to zedoary, gives botanical information, medical properties, folklore, economic uses, much else. Indispensable to serious reader. 161 illustrations. 888pp. 6½ x 9¼. 2-vol. set. (Available in U.S. only.) Vol. I: 0-486-22798-7 Vol. II: 0-486-22799-5

HIDDEN TREASURE MAZE BOOK, Dave Phillips. Solve 34 challenging mazes accompanied by heroic tales of adventure. Evil dragons, people-eating plants, blood-thirsty giants, many more dangerous adversaries lurk at every twist and turn. 34 mazes, stories, solutions. 48pp. 8¼ x 11. 0-486-24566-7

LETTERS OF W. A. MOZART, Wolfgang A. Mozart. Remarkable letters show bawdy wit, humor, imagination, musical insights, contemporary musical world; includes some letters from Leopold Mozart. 276pp. 5⅜ x 8½. 0-486-22859-2

BASIC PRINCIPLES OF CLASSICAL BALLET, Agrippina Vaganova. Great Russian theoretician, teacher explains methods for teaching classical ballet. 118 illustrations. 175pp. 5⅜ x 8½. 0-486-22036-2

THE JUMPING FROG, Mark Twain. Revenge edition. The original story of The Celebrated Jumping Frog of Calaveras County, a hapless French translation, and Twain's hilarious "retranslation" from the French. 12 illustrations. 66pp. 5⅜ x 8½. 0-486-22686-7

BEST REMEMBERED POEMS, Martin Gardner (ed.). The 126 poems in this superb collection of 19th- and 20th-century British and American verse range from Shelley's "To a Skylark" to the impassioned "Renascence" of Edna St. Vincent Millay and to Edward Lear's whimsical "The Owl and the Pussycat." 224pp. 5⅜ x 8½. 0-486-27165-X

COMPLETE SONNETS, William Shakespeare. Over 150 exquisite poems deal with love, friendship, the tyranny of time, beauty's evanescence, death and other themes in language of remarkable power, precision and beauty. Glossary of archaic terms. 80pp. $5\frac{3}{16}$ x 8¼. 0-486-26686-9

HISTORIC HOMES OF THE AMERICAN PRESIDENTS, Second, Revised Edition, Irvin Haas. A traveler's guide to American Presidential homes, most open to the public, depicting and describing homes occupied by every American President from George Washington to George Bush. With visiting hours, admission charges, travel routes. 175 photographs. Index. 160pp. 8¼ x 11. 0-486-26751-2

THE WIT AND HUMOR OF OSCAR WILDE, Alvin Redman (ed.). More than 1,000 ripostes, paradoxes, wisecracks: Work is the curse of the drinking classes; I can resist everything except temptation; etc. 258pp. 5⅜ x 8½. 0-486-20602-5

SHAKESPEARE LEXICON AND QUOTATION DICTIONARY, Alexander Schmidt. Full definitions, locations, shades of meaning in every word in plays and poems. More than 50,000 exact quotations. 1,485pp. 6½ x 9¼. 2-vol. set. Vol. 1: 0-486-22726-X Vol. 2: 0-486-22727-8

SELECTED POEMS, Emily Dickinson. Over 100 best-known, best-loved poems by one of America's foremost poets, reprinted from authoritative early editions. No comparable edition at this price. Index of first lines. 64pp. $5\frac{3}{16}$ x 8¼. 0-486-26466-1

THE INSIDIOUS DR. FU-MANCHU, Sax Rohmer. The first of the popular mystery series introduces a pair of English detectives to their archnemesis, the diabolical Dr. Fu-Manchu. Flavorful atmosphere, fast-paced action, and colorful characters enliven this classic of the genre. 208pp. $5\frac{3}{16}$ x 8¼. 0-486-29898-1

THE MALLEUS MALEFICARUM OF KRAMER AND SPRENGER, translated by Montague Summers. Full text of most important witchhunter's "bible," used by both Catholics and Protestants. 278pp. 6⅝ x 10. 0-486-22802-9

SPANISH STORIES/CUENTOS ESPAÑOLES: A Dual-Language Book, Angel Flores (ed.). Unique format offers 13 great stories in Spanish by Cervantes, Borges, others. Faithful English translations on facing pages. 352pp. 5⅜ x 8½. 0-486-25399-6

GARDEN CITY, LONG ISLAND, IN EARLY PHOTOGRAPHS, 1869–1919, Mildred H. Smith. Handsome treasury of 118 vintage pictures, accompanied by carefully researched captions, document the Garden City Hotel fire (1899), the Vanderbilt Cup Race (1908), the first airmail flight departing from the Nassau Boulevard Aerodrome (1911), and much more. 96pp. 8⅞ x 11¾. 0-486-40669-5

OLD QUEENS, N.Y., IN EARLY PHOTOGRAPHS, Vincent F. Seyfried and William Asadorian. Over 160 rare photographs of Maspeth, Jamaica, Jackson Heights, and other areas. Vintage views of DeWitt Clinton mansion, 1939 World's Fair and more. Captions. 192pp. 8⅞ x 11. 0-486-26358-4

CAPTURED BY THE INDIANS: 15 Firsthand Accounts, 1750-1870, Frederick Drimmer. Astounding true historical accounts of grisly torture, bloody conflicts, relentless pursuits, miraculous escapes and more, by people who lived to tell the tale. 384pp. 5⅜ x 8½. 0-486-24901-8

THE WORLD'S GREAT SPEECHES (Fourth Enlarged Edition), Lewis Copeland, Lawrence W. Lamm, and Stephen J. McKenna. Nearly 300 speeches provide public speakers with a wealth of updated quotes and inspiration—from Pericles' funeral oration and William Jennings Bryan's "Cross of Gold Speech" to Malcolm X's powerful words on the Black Revolution and Earl of Spenser's tribute to his sister, Diana, Princess of Wales. 944pp. 5⅜ x 8⅜. 0-486-40903-1

THE BOOK OF THE SWORD, Sir Richard F. Burton. Great Victorian scholar/adventurer's eloquent, erudite history of the "queen of weapons"—from prehistory to early Roman Empire. Evolution and development of early swords, variations (sabre, broadsword, cutlass, scimitar, etc.), much more. 336pp. 6⅛ x 9¼. 0-486-25434-8

AUTOBIOGRAPHY: The Story of My Experiments with Truth, Mohandas K. Gandhi. Boyhood, legal studies, purification, the growth of the Satyagraha (nonviolent protest) movement. Critical, inspiring work of the man responsible for the freedom of India. 480pp. 5⅜ x 8½. (Available in U.S. only.) 0-486-24593-4

CELTIC MYTHS AND LEGENDS, T. W. Rolleston. Masterful retelling of Irish and Welsh stories and tales. Cuchulain, King Arthur, Deirdre, the Grail, many more. First paperback edition. 58 full-page illustrations. 512pp. 5⅜ x 8½. 0-486-26507-2

THE PRINCIPLES OF PSYCHOLOGY, William James. Famous long course complete, unabridged. Stream of thought, time perception, memory, experimental methods; great work decades ahead of its time. 94 figures. 1,391pp. 5⅜ x 8½. 2-vol. set.
Vol. I: 0-486-20381-6   Vol. II: 0-486-20382-4

THE WORLD AS WILL AND REPRESENTATION, Arthur Schopenhauer. Definitive English translation of Schopenhauer's life work, correcting more than 1,000 errors, omissions in earlier translations. Translated by E. F. J. Payne. Total of 1,269pp. 5⅜ x 8½. 2-vol. set.   Vol. 1: 0-486-21761-2   Vol. 2: 0-486-21762-0

MAGIC AND MYSTERY IN TIBET, Madame Alexandra David-Neel. Experiences among lamas, magicians, sages, sorcerers, Bonpa wizards. A true psychic discovery. 32 illustrations. 321pp. 5⅜ x 8½. (Available in U.S. only.)   0-486-22682-4

THE EGYPTIAN BOOK OF THE DEAD, E. A. Wallis Budge. Complete reproduction of Ani's papyrus, finest ever found. Full hieroglyphic text, interlinear transliteration, word-for-word translation, smooth translation. 533pp. 6½ x 9¼.
0-486-21866-X

HISTORIC COSTUME IN PICTURES, Braun & Schneider. Over 1,450 costumed figures in clearly detailed engravings—from dawn of civilization to end of 19th century. Captions. Many folk costumes. 256pp. 8⅜ x 11¾.   0-486-23150-X

MATHEMATICS FOR THE NONMATHEMATICIAN, Morris Kline. Detailed, college-level treatment of mathematics in cultural and historical context, with numerous exercises. Recommended Reading Lists. Tables. Numerous figures. 641pp. 5⅜ x 8½.
0-486-24823-2

PROBABILISTIC METHODS IN THE THEORY OF STRUCTURES, Isaac Elishakoff. Well-written introduction covers the elements of the theory of probability from two or more random variables, the reliability of such multivariable structures, the theory of random function, Monte Carlo methods of treating problems incapable of exact solution, and more. Examples. 502pp. 5⅜ x 8½.   0-486-40691-1

THE RIME OF THE ANCIENT MARINER, Gustave Doré, S. T. Coleridge. Doré's finest work; 34 plates capture moods, subtleties of poem. Flawless full-size reproductions printed on facing pages with authoritative text of poem. "Beautiful. Simply beautiful."—*Publisher's Weekly.* 77pp. 9¼ x 12.   0-486-22305-1

SCULPTURE: Principles and Practice, Louis Slobodkin. Step-by-step approach to clay, plaster, metals, stone; classical and modern. 253 drawings, photos. 255pp. 8⅛ x 11.
0-486-22960-2

THE INFLUENCE OF SEA POWER UPON HISTORY, 1660–1783, A. T. Mahan. Influential classic of naval history and tactics still used as text in war colleges. First paperback edition. 4 maps. 24 battle plans. 640pp. 5⅜ x 8½.   0-486-25509-3

THE STORY OF THE TITANIC AS TOLD BY ITS SURVIVORS, Jack Winocour (ed.). What it was really like. Panic, despair, shocking inefficiency, and a little heroism. More thrilling than any fictional account. 26 illustrations. 320pp. 5⅜ x 8½.
0-486-20610-6

ONE TWO THREE . . . INFINITY: Facts and Speculations of Science, George Gamow. Great physicist's fascinating, readable overview of contemporary science: number theory, relativity, fourth dimension, entropy, genes, atomic structure, much more. 128 illustrations. Index. 352pp. 5⅜ x 8½.   0-486-25664-2

DALÍ ON MODERN ART: The Cuckolds of Antiquated Modern Art, Salvador Dalí. Influential painter skewers modern art and its practitioners. Outrageous evaluations of Picasso, Cézanne, Turner, more. 15 renderings of paintings discussed. 44 calligraphic decorations by Dalí. 96pp. 5⅜ x 8½. (Available in U.S. only.)   0-486-29220-7

ANTIQUE PLAYING CARDS: A Pictorial History, Henry René D'Allemagne. Over 900 elaborate, decorative images from rare playing cards (14th–20th centuries): Bacchus, death, dancing dogs, hunting scenes, royal coats of arms, players cheating, much more. 96pp. 9¼ x 12¼.   0-486-29265-7

MAKING FURNITURE MASTERPIECES: 30 Projects with Measured Drawings, Franklin H. Gottshall. Step-by-step instructions, illustrations for constructing handsome, useful pieces, among them a Sheraton desk, Chippendale chair, Spanish desk, Queen Anne table and a William and Mary dressing mirror. 224pp. 8⅛ x 11¼. 0-486-29338-6

NORTH AMERICAN INDIAN DESIGNS FOR ARTISTS AND CRAFTSPEOPLE, Eva Wilson. Over 360 authentic copyright-free designs adapted from Navajo blankets, Hopi pottery, Sioux buffalo hides, more. Geometrics, symbolic figures, plant and animal motifs, etc. 128pp. 8⅜ x 11. (Not for sale in the United Kingdom.) 0-486-25341-4

THE FOSSIL BOOK: A Record of Prehistoric Life, Patricia V. Rich et al. Profusely illustrated definitive guide covers everything from single-celled organisms and dinosaurs to birds and mammals and the interplay between climate and man. Over 1,500 illustrations. 760pp. 7½ x 10⅛. 0-486-29371-8

VICTORIAN ARCHITECTURAL DETAILS: Designs for Over 700 Stairs, Mantels, Doors, Windows, Cornices, Porches, and Other Decorative Elements, A. J. Bicknell & Company. Everything from dormer windows and piazzas to balconies and gable ornaments. Also includes elevations and floor plans for handsome, private residences and commercial structures. 80pp. 9⅜ x 12¼. 0-486-44015-X

WESTERN ISLAMIC ARCHITECTURE: A Concise Introduction, John D. Hoag. Profusely illustrated critical appraisal compares and contrasts Islamic mosques and palaces—from Spain and Egypt to other areas in the Middle East. 139 illustrations. 128pp. 6 x 9. 0-486-43760-4

CHINESE ARCHITECTURE: A Pictorial History, Liang Ssu-ch'eng. More than 240 rare photographs and drawings depict temples, pagodas, tombs, bridges, and imperial palaces comprising much of China's architectural heritage. 152 halftones, 94 diagrams. 232pp. 10¾ x 9⅞. 0-486-43999-2

THE RENAISSANCE: Studies in Art and Poetry, Walter Pater. One of the most talked-about books of the 19th century, *The Renaissance* combines scholarship and philosophy in an innovative work of cultural criticism that examines the achievements of Botticelli, Leonardo, Michelangelo, and other artists. "The holy writ of beauty."—Oscar Wilde. 160pp. 5⅜ x 8½. 0-486-44025-7

A TREATISE ON PAINTING, Leonardo da Vinci. The great Renaissance artist's practical advice on drawing and painting techniques covers anatomy, perspective, composition, light and shadow, and color. A classic of art instruction, it features 48 drawings by Nicholas Poussin and Leon Battista Alberti. 192pp. 5⅜ x 8½. 0-486-44155-5

THE MIND OF LEONARDO DA VINCI, Edward McCurdy. More than just a biography, this classic study by a distinguished historian draws upon Leonardo's extensive writings to offer numerous demonstrations of the Renaissance master's achievements, not only in sculpture and painting, but also in music, engineering, and even experimental aviation. 384pp. 5⅜ x 8½. 0-486-44142-3

WASHINGTON IRVING'S RIP VAN WINKLE, Illustrated by Arthur Rackham. Lovely prints that established artist as a leading illustrator of the time and forever etched into the popular imagination a classic of Catskill lore. 51 full-color plates. 80pp. 8⅜ x 11. 0-486-44242-X

HENSCHE ON PAINTING, John W. Robichaux. Basic painting philosophy and methodology of a great teacher, as expounded in his famous classes and workshops on Cape Cod. 7 illustrations in color on covers. 80pp. 5⅜ x 8½. 0-486-43728-0

CATALOG OF DOVER BOOKS

LIGHT AND SHADE: A Classic Approach to Three-Dimensional Drawing, Mrs. Mary P. Merrifield. Handy reference clearly demonstrates principles of light and shade by revealing effects of common daylight, sunshine, and candle or artificial light on geometrical solids. 13 plates. 64pp. 5⅜ x 8½. 0-486-44143-1

ASTROLOGY AND ASTRONOMY: A Pictorial Archive of Signs and Symbols, Ernst and Johanna Lehner. Treasure trove of stories, lore, and myth, accompanied by more than 300 rare illustrations of planets, the Milky Way, signs of the zodiac, comets, meteors, and other astronomical phenomena. 192pp. 8⅜ x 11. 0-486-43981-X

JEWELRY MAKING: Techniques for Metal, Tim McCreight. Easy-to-follow instructions and carefully executed illustrations describe tools and techniques, use of gems and enamels, wire inlay, casting, and other topics. 72 line illustrations and diagrams. 176pp. 8¼ x 10⅞. 0-486-44043-5

MAKING BIRDHOUSES: Easy and Advanced Projects, Gladstone Califf. Easy-to-follow instructions include diagrams for everything from a one-room house for bluebirds to a forty-two-room structure for purple martins. 56 plates; 4 figures. 80pp. 8¾ x 6⅜. 0-486-44183-0

LITTLE BOOK OF LOG CABINS: How to Build and Furnish Them, William S. Wicks. Handy how-to manual, with instructions and illustrations for building cabins in the Adirondack style, fireplaces, stairways, furniture, beamed ceilings, and more. 102 line drawings. 96pp. 8¾ x 6⅜. 0-486-44259-4

THE SEASONS OF AMERICA PAST, Eric Sloane. From "sugaring time" and strawberry picking to Indian summer and fall harvest, a whole year's activities described in charming prose and enhanced with 79 of the author's own illustrations. 160pp. 8¼ x 11. 0-486-44220-9

THE METROPOLIS OF TOMORROW, Hugh Ferriss. Generous, prophetic vision of the metropolis of the future, as perceived in 1929. Powerful illustrations of towering structures, wide avenues, and rooftop parks–all features in many of today's modern cities. 59 illustrations. 144pp. 8¼ x 11. 0-486-43727-2

THE PATH TO ROME, Hilaire Belloc. This 1902 memoir abounds in lively vignettes from a vanished time, recounting a pilgrimage on foot across the Alps and Apennines in order to "see all Europe which the Christian Faith has saved." 77 of the author's original line drawings complement his sparkling prose. 272pp. 5⅜ x 8½. 0-486-44001-X

THE HISTORY OF RASSELAS: Prince of Abissinia, Samuel Johnson. Distinguished English writer attacks eighteenth-century optimism and man's unrealistic estimates of what life has to offer. 112pp. 5⅜ x 8½. 0-486-44094-X

A VOYAGE TO ARCTURUS, David Lindsay. A brilliant flight of pure fancy, where wild creatures crowd the fantastic landscape and demented torturers dominate victims with their bizarre mental powers. 272pp. 5⅜ x 8½. 0-486-44198-9

Paperbound unless otherwise indicated. Available at your book dealer, online at **www.doverpublications.com**, or by writing to Dept. GI, Dover Publications, Inc., 31 East 2nd Street, Mineola, NY 11501. For current price information or for free catalogs (please indicate field of interest), write to Dover Publications or log on to **www.doverpublications.com** and see every Dover book in print. Dover publishes more than 500 books each year on science, elementary and advanced mathematics, biology, music, art, literary history, social sciences, and other areas.